SMILEY BURNETTE
We Called Him Frog

by
Bobby J. Copeland
and
Richard B. Smith, III

Published by:
Empire Publishing, Inc.
3130 US Highway 220
Madison, NC 27025-8306
Phone: 336-427-5850 • Fax: 336-427-7372
Email: info@empirepublishinginc.com

Other books by Bobby J. Copeland:
Trail Talk, published by Empire Publishing
B-Western Boot Hill, published by Empire Publishing
Bill Elliott — The Peaceable Man, published by Empire Publishing
Roy Barcroft — King of the Badmen, published by Empire Publishing
Charlie King — We Called Him Blackie, published by Empire Publishing
Silent Hoofbeats, published by Empire Publishing
Johnny Mack Brown — Up Close and Personal, published by Empire Publishing
The Bob Baker Story, published by BoJo Enterprises
The Whip Wilson Story, published by BoJo Enterprises
Five Heroes, published by BoJo Enterprises
The Tom Tyler Story (Mike Chapman and Bobby Copeland), published by Culture House Books
Best of the Badmen by Boyd Magers, Bob Nareau and Bobby Copeland, published by Empire Publishing
Sunset Carson —The Adventures of a Cowboy Hero, published by Empire Publishing

Empire Publishing, Inc.
3130 US Highway 220
Madison, NC 27025-8306
Phone: 336-427-5850
Fax: 336-427-7372
Email: info@empirepublishinginc.com

Smiley Burnette — We Called Him Frog © 2007 by Bobby J. Copeland and Richard B. Smith, III

All rights reserved under International and Pan American copyright convention. No part of this book may be reproduced in any manner whatsoever without written permission from the publisher, except in the case of brief quotations embodied in reviews and articles.

Library of Congress Catalog Number 2007938476
ISBN Number 978-0944019-51-1

Published and printed in the United States of America
1 2 3 4 5 5 6 7 8 9 10

ACKNOWLEDGMENTS

Thanks to the following Individuals:

Les Adams
Grady Franklin
Boyd Magers
Larry Hopper
Ken Jones
Bill Russell
Mike Marx
Jim Kocher
Hans Wolstein
Clint Mitchell
Doug Morris
Joe Copeland
Ralph Absher
Ross Pittman
O. J. Sikes
Bill Sasser
Doneen Key
Don Key
Rhonda Lemons
Billy Weathersby
Don Calhoun
Larry Welch
Mack Houston
The staff of the Margaret Herrick Library of AMPAS

TABLE OF CONTENTS

Meet Smiley Burnette   7
Smiley Speaks   24
Frog's Friends   28
Frog Friction   34
Frugal Frog   38
They're Writing About Smiley   41
Western Film Fans Speak   47
Frog's Fan Club   58
Smiley the Songster   64
Burnette and John Cason   71
Smiley Snippets   72
Pat Buttram and the Cannon   77
Gene Autry on Strike   80
Popularity Rankings of Smiley   89
Burnette at Republic and Columbia   90
Smiley's Film Roles   101
Dual Roles   165
Obituary   170
Selected Bibliography   171
About the Authors   172

MEET SMILEY BURNETTE

Smiley "Frog" Burnette has been described by critics as anywhere from a comic and musical genius to a babbling, obnoxious buffoon. One thing for certain, Smiley influenced the course of Western comedy. However, comedy is a personal thing—what is funny to some may not be funny to others. For sure, he did popularize the role of the Western sidekick and made it of an importance nearly equal to that of the star. And there is no question that he was a multi-talented instrumentalist and prolific songwriter. While he had his detractors, many others consider him to be one of the most beloved performers to appear in B-Westerns.

Smiley's clowning went over extremely well with Gene Autry, but it often did not work so well with the other cowboys, especially in the Charles Starrett *Durango Kid* series. Possibly, his comedy was better with Autry because they were friends, and Autry was a willing participant in Smiley's antics. Others, like Starrett, would simply leave the set when it came time for Smiley go into his act.

Lester Alvin Burnette is remembered by many Western fans as Smiley Burnette. However, to most fans, he is best known and best loved for his characterization of "Frog Millhouse." Burnette was born to George Washington Burnett (this was original spelling) and Almira Heslip Burnett in Summum, Illinois, on March 18, 1911. Both parents were co-ministers in the

Christian Church. The family relocated to Monticello, Illinois, when Smiley was very young.

Burnette had an early fascination for music and could play almost any instrument he got his hands on. Supposedly, his first performance was at the age of nine at a Y.M.C.A. function.

He hated his first name because the other school children would call him "Lester the pester." Smiley would chide them and say, "If you want to be my friend, don't call me Lester!"

Contrary to many reports, Smiley did not finish high school. He dropped out of Astoria (Illinois) High School in the ninth grade to help support his family. He held various menial jobs until he found work on the tiny 100-watt radio station, WDZ, in Tuscola, Illinois. Burnette described his job: "I did about ten shows a day, using a different name on each one so folks would think they were listening to different people. My name was 'Mr. Smiley' on the children's show."

How did Lester Burnette become Smiley Burnette? The story goes that Smiley was reading Mark Twain's *Jumping Frog of Calaveras County* and came across a character called Reverend Lionidas W. Smiley. Since he was now doing a radio kid's program, and since he did not want to be called Lester, he decided to call himself Mr. Smiley. Later the "Mr." was dropped and the name "Smiley" was born. It is quite likely he also chose the name "Frog" from the title of the Twain story. However, the "Frog Millhouse" name did not occur until the 1935 Republic film, MELODY TRAIL.

It was while working at the small station in Tuscola that it became Smiley's good fortune to receive a telephone call from recording star, and station WLS Chicago entertainer, Gene Autry. In Autry's autobiography, *Back in the Saddle Again*, he tells of hiring Smiley:

> "We were short a musician on a tour of the Midwest. We were playing at Champaign-Urbana in a theater near the

University of Illinois, and I asked the manager if he knew where I could find an accordion player. He said 'Why yes, there is a young fellow down the road at Tuscola, about 25 miles south of here. He works for a radio station. Plays the piano, guitar, and sings. Has lots of talent.' He gave me the name Smiley Burnette and the number of the station. I got him on the phone, told him who I was, and said brightly, 'I hear you play the accordion.' He said, 'Yup, I sure do.' I asked him how much he was making at the station. 'Eighteen dollars a week,' he said. 'I'll pay you fifty,' I told him, 'plus your expenses on the road. You think it about it and if you want to come with us let me know.' He said, 'I just thought about it. You done hired yourself an accordion player.'"

Smiley, laughingly, described his first year with Gene: "It wasn't a big year in money for me, but I learned more from Autry than I can say. Whenever the wolf came to the door—Autry ended up with a fur coat."

Gene and Smiley made their first joint appearance on the WLS National Barn Dance on Christmas Eve, 1933. The station was owned by the Sears and Roebuck Company, and the call letters, WLS, stood for the "World's Largest Store."

A few months later Nat Levine, head of Mascot Studios, contacted Autry about coming to Hollywood. At the time, Smiley was under a personal contract to Autry. So when it became apparent Gene was leaving for California, Burnette encouraged Autry to make him part of the deal rather than trying to persuade WLS to pick up his contract. Although it has been reported that Burnette was signed to a picture contract anywhere from $500 to a $1,000 a week—actually it was only for $35. (Autry was paid $100 a week.) The $35 for Smiley certainly makes more sense since, a few years later (October 13, 1937), Roy Rogers was signed as a leading Republic cowboy star for $75 per week under term contract.

Autry and Burnette had small parts in Ken Maynard's IN OLD

SANTA FE (Mascot, 1934) and then headed back east. The movie proved to be a hit. One theater owner in Louisiana wrote about the picture: "A good Western with plenty of music and fun. Not the usual shoot 'em up and drag out type, just a good comical modern Western. Give us more of this type." Although Autry and Burnette were not mentioned by name, obviously the owner was referring to their contributions to the movie.

According to Gene, he was surprised when he and Smiley were called back to Hollywood to make the serial, THE PHANTOM EMPIRE (Mascot, 1935). Burnette was billed as "Oscar" in the serial.

In Autry's first feature, TUMBLING TUMBLEWEEDS (Republic, 1935), Burnette was called "Smiley." It was in Gene's second feature MELODY TRAIL (Republic, 1935) (Mascot had now become Republic), when the name "Frog Millhouse" first appeared.

Smiley soon discovered that, during his riding scenes, he had trouble keeping his black cowboy hat on. He then turned up the hat's brim to keep the wind from dislodging the hat. Later, when he saw himself in the mirror with the newly styled hat, he thought it a perfect fit for his role as "Frog," so he pinned it up permanently. Other comics who sometimes copied Smiley's hat style include Gabby Hayes, Fuzzy St. John, Raymond Hatton, Slim Andrews, Dub Taylor and Horace Murphy.

Smiley is one of the few sidekicks who did not use profanity, tobacco or alcohol. Other sidekicks who at one time had been known to be heavy drinkers include Fuzzy Knight, Fuzzy St. John, Dub Taylor, Lasses White, Cliff Edwards, and Emmett Lynn.

No one, including the Republic officials, could have predicted the phenomenal popularity of the Autry/Burnette pictures. The success was instantaneous and proved to be one of the most popular series ever made—certainly the most popular Western series.

In 1936, a theater owner in Nelsonville, Ohio, commented on

the popularity of the films:

> *Autry's Westerns, TUMBLING TUMBLEWEEDS, MELODY TRAIL, and SAGEBRUSH TROUBADOUR, are the outstanding pictures of the season. They are tops in all ways. Give these pictures your preferred playing time and watch the crowds roll in. As business getters these pictures are ahead of Cantor (Eddie), Astaire (Fred) and Rogers (Ginger), and a lot of other big stars. Republic sells these pictures at just a rental so as to leave you a profit. I had more profit on TUMBLING TUMBLEWEEDS than I did on TOP HAT (a 1935 RKO picture with Fred Astaire and Ginger Rogers). People came to see this picture I have never seen in the theater before—and they left satisfied.*

Another theater owner in Anamosa, Pennsylvania, wrote: "Anyone who passes up Autry misses a good bet. He is one of the best moneymakers for smaller towns. What do we care about the cost (low-budget) of production? Autry with Smiley gets them in and they love it and we take the gate receipts."

The late Alex Gordon, a long time business associate of Autry, explained the difference in the Autry/Burnette pictures vs. other B-Westerns: "Gene introduced an entirely different format with music logically worked into the plots, but still showing problems with cattle disease, flood, droughts, dust storms, Native American problems and more. Also, the women were feisty, not helpless heroines as before. They often gave Gene a real 'Taming of the Shrew' type situation. Women writers wrote many of the scripts."

Gene and Smiley had only been settled in Hollywood for a short time when Gene helped to provide the needed funds for moving Smiley's parents to California, where they continued their ministry.

In 1936, Reb Russell held a picnic in honor of newspaper columnist Dallas MacDonnell, who had written a nice article

Gene and Smiley cheerily pose during a 1937 Republic publicity shot for one of the Autry movies.

about the cowboy star. Smiley and Gene lived near Russell and were invited to the picnic. The columnist took an instant liking to the outgoing Burnette, and although she was 12 years his senior, they began dating. Before long a December wedding was planned, but the plans were scrapped when the couple decided to elope. They were wed on October 26, 1936, while Smiley was filming THE OLD CORRAL (Republic, 1936). The marriage was a good one and endured until Smiley's death. He and Dallas adopted four children—all from Tennessee. The four children, from oldest to youngest, were Linda, Stephen, Carolyn, and Brian.

(Stephen Burnette spent 16 years as a member of LOCAL 729, Motion Picture Set Painter and Sign Writer, working for various productions. He entered the movie business as a child. Smiley would place Stephen in scenes of Westerns on which he was working. In 1963, Stephen became an actor and stuntman and remained in front of the camera, and with productions,

until 1989. One of the films in which he did stunts was 1985's SILVERADO, starring Kevin Costner.)

After 20 highly successful Autry/Burnette features, Gene realized the tremendous profits Republic was making on his films and wanted the studio to share some of those revenues with him. He discovered negotiating with Republic czar Herbert J. Yates was no easy task. Since the studio would not give in to his demands, Gene decided to go on strike. Immediately, Republic set out to obtain an injunction to stop him from performing elsewhere. *(Note: See the section titled GENE AUTRY ON STRIKE.)*

Republic then tried to hire Tex Ritter, another singing cowboy, to replace the striking Autry. At the time, Ritter was making a series of movies for Grand National. Unfortunately, for Ritter, he was under a contract to producer Ed Finney. When Republic learned Finney would have to be part of the deal, the studio decided to go in a different direction and hired Roy Rogers for its new Western singing star.

If Republic had been successful in hiring Tex Ritter, undoubtedly, Smiley (who did not strike with Autry), would have become Ritter's sidekick. The easygoing Ritter and the affable Burnette would have made an interesting match-up. The move away from lowly Grand National to Republic would have been a tremendous break for Ritter, and Smiley would have been a definite improvement over the sidekicks tossed into the Ritter films.

With Gene Autry on strike, and with Burnette available, Republic decided to give its newcomer star Roy Rogers a boost by putting Burnette in Roy's initial film, UNDER WESTERN STARS (1938). Since Rogers was virtually unknown, and since Smiley had been extremely popular with movie audiences in the Autry series, there is no question that Smiley proved a valuable asset in jump-starting the Rogers series.

Smiley is often credited with naming Roy Rogers' horse Trigger, but did he? Roy always said, "The name came up when we were getting ready to do the first picture. Smiley Burnette and I and some others who were there got to kicking it around while I was fooling around with my guns as we talked. I *believe* it was actually Smiley Burnette who said, 'As fast and as quick as the horse is, you ought to call him Trigger. You know, quick-on-the-trigger.' I said, 'That's a good name.' And I just named him Trigger." *(It is important to note that Roy said, "I believe it was Smiley" — he did not say for sure that Smiley named Trigger.)*

Joe Kane, who directed 42 of Roy's movies, including UNDER WESTERN STARS, stated emphatically that it was he who named the soon to be famous steed: "While we were on location on that picture, they sent word up that he was going to be called Roy Rogers (he had been using the name Dick Weston), and they wanted a name for his horse. We were getting ready to shoot a scene with a revolver, so I said, 'Why don't we call him Trigger?' They took that name, and he became Trigger."

The premier of UNDER WESTERN STARS was held in April 1938, in Dallas, Texas, with Roy, Smiley, and The Sons of the Pioneers present for a stage show prior to the showing of the movie.

Although Smiley had not joined Gene in the strike, he may have joined the singing cowboy if the pair had accepted a proposal to tour in South America. *The New York Times* reported the following on May 3, 1938:

> *This week Autry found a solution, if only temporarily, for his troubles* (the injunction). *The court order is unenforceable in South America and Juan Castillo has offered him a 20-week tour for which the star will receive $4,000 a week and his screen partner, Smiley Burnette, will be paid $1,000. Western stars are popular in Latin American countries and Castillo feels that he can make a small fortune during the five months. The engagement will give Autry the equivalent of two years' salary with Republic, will keep him before a portion of*

his public, and will make a possible prolonged battle with the studio if that is necessary.

Since Autry and Republic soon reached an agreement on a new contract, the South American tour never happened. With the contract now settled, Gene and Smiley resumed filming on May 21, 1938 with GOLD MINE IN THE SKY (Republic, 1938). One stipulation in Gene's new contract was that Smiley would appear exclusively in Gene Autry's movies.

In 1940, Smiley, for the first time in five years, missed out on being Autry's sidekick in MELODY RANCH. Gabby Hayes did have a large part in the film. According to an article by Louella Parsons in the August 22, 1940, *Washington Post*, producer Sol Siegel did not want Smiley teamed with Autry for this picture because he feared the audience would think it was a routine Autry/Burnette film and would not recoup the studio's large investment in project. This is why Jimmy Durante was in the picture instead of Burnette. During this time, Smiley's contract with Republic was renewed.

Not everyone was pleased with Siegel's decision of not using Smiley in MELODY RANCH. N. E. Frank, a movie exhibitor in Wayland, Michigan, wrote of Smiley's absence in the picture: "The fans missed Smiley Burnette. Taking Smiley away from Gene is like taking the motor out of your car."

Western film historian Boyd Magers said of the picture:

> *Supposedly planned as a pivotal film in Gene Autry's career, Republic budgeted this turkey at $180,000, the most expensive Autry to date. Sporting a huge cast headed by veteran comedian Jimmy Durante (replacing Autry favorite Smiley Burnette), the vaudeville trouper's gnarled phraseology comic antics—especially an extended courtroom scene—proved unfunny and out of place in an Autry film. Durante was not appreciated by Autry fans that preferred Smiley's homespun humor.*

It was also in 1940 that Burnette developed Bell's palsy. The disease left him with a right eye that appeared swollen or unfocused throughout the rest of his screen appearances. *(Bell's palsy is sudden weakness or paralysis of the muscles on one side of the face due to malfunction of cranial nerve VII (facial nerve), which stimulates the facial muscles.)*

"TADPOLE" JOINS SMILEY AND GENE

Joe "Tadpole" Strauch Jr. (1929 -1986), a "Frog Millhouse" look- and dress-a-like, joined the Autry/Burnette series for five films starting with UNDER FIESTA STARS (Republic, 1941). Many feel he was not a welcome addition. Earlier, Strauch had been a stand-in for "Spanky" McFarland at Hal Roach Studios for the "Our Gang" comedies. He later played the role of "Tubby" in a 1941 MGM "Our Gang" episode. Strauch turned in his finest performance in UNDER FIESTA STARS. In the film, he played Smiley's brother. At other times, he was Smiley's nephew.

Apparently, some studios, including Republic, felt that since the films were primarily directed to juveniles, the movie-going youngsters would enjoy seeing children of their age in the movies. This was not the case. Young performers like Strauch, Twinkle Watts, Sugar Dawn, and others were tried with little or no success. The only regular child actor in a B-Western series that was generally accepted by the young audience was Bobby "Little Beaver" Blake in Republic's *Red Ryder* movies. Although not appearing regularly in a series, little Sammy McKim was enjoyable to watch.

After Gene Autry volunteered for the service in 1942, Republic kept Burnette busy by casting him in films with Roy Rogers, Eddie Dew, Bob Livingston and Sunset Carson. He worked well with Rogers, but his work with the other cowboys was uninspiring.

In order to jump-start the Sunset Carson series at Republic (like the studio had done earlier with Roy Rogers), it cast Burnette

Gene Autry, Smiley Burnette, and Joe Strauch Jr. take a camera break on BELLS OF CAPISTRANO (Republic, 1942).

with him. And due to Burnette's popularity at the time, he was billed over Carson. Smiley worked in four 1944 pictures with Carson, and then he and Republic parted company. While at Republic, his usual stand-in was movie badman Tex Terry.

(A stand-in substitutes for the star during the tedious process of preparing scenes, setting up the camera, taking light-meter readings, adjusting lights, etc. He is chosen due to his physical resemblance of the star. The stand-in may occasionally be used as substitute for the star in long shots and crowd scenes

where no acting is required. When a stand-in is used in potentially hazardous situations or stunts requiring physically agility, he is better known as a double.)

Smiley did some decent work in the Livingston pictures, except for BENEATH WESTERN SKIES (Republic, 1944). In this film, Joe "Tadpole" Strauch Jr. shows up again to work with Burnette. A further distraction was an atrocious looking

A photo montage of Gene Autry in various stages of his B-Western career at Republic and Columbia Studios.

dummy, operated by Burnette, called "Toad." (Audiences now had a "Frog," a "Tadpole," and a "Toad.") This led to way too much buffoonery and not enough Livingston. As far as can be determined, Livingston and Burnette were the first Western hero and sidekick to both ride white horses. The trend continued when Smiley worked with Sunset Carson.

SMILEY LEAVES REPUBLIC

Since Republic owned the use of the names "Frog Millhouse" and "Black-Eyed Nellie" (Burnette's horse), both names ended after the 1944 Sunset Carson feature FIREBRANDS OF ARIZONA. When Burnette joined Charles Starrett for *The Durango Kid* features in 1945, he was billed as "Smiley Burnette" and his horse was called "Ringeye."

Why did Smiley leave Republic? There has been much speculation as to why he left the studio. Some claim he was fired. Many have written that he left for more money to join Starrett at Columbia. The latter theory does not hold water since Burnette did not make films for 10 months. The truth is revealed by the late Republic guru Jack Mathis in his excellently researched book, *Republic Confidential — The Studio*: Mathis reports that Smiley requested, and was granted, a release from his contract in 1944. Since he was making $1,000 a week (when working), and since he had not been very successful in his roles without Autry, Republic was probably more than willing to honor his request. Did Smiley think, because he had received top billing over newcomer Sunset Carson, that he was now a hot item and another studio would immediately come calling? If so, he was badly mistaken. And it is highly probable that Columbia paid him more than he had been making at Republic.

In the Starrett series, Smiley was billed as "The West's No. 1 Comic." There is no question that Smiley worked hard in the Starrett features, but his attempt at comedy was often unfunny. And, at times, it was ridiculous. Since Starrett was usually not present during Burnette's parts, some have suggested the films would be more enjoyable by cutting Smiley's antics from them. Another thing that bothers many Starrett fans is that Smiley was often given more screen time than the star.

Bob Carmen and Dan Scapperotti wrote in their fine book, *The Adventures of the Durango Kid,* about Smiley's participation in the Starrett features:

> Burnette's comedy touches had their place and were a plus factor in many of the films. There were times, however, when his antics were so broad that they weren't funny. One scene in TRAIL TO LAREDO (Columbia, 1948) finds the comedian trying to paint and paper a saloon wall while an intense card game is in progress. The players are pelted with paint, paste, and wallpaper by the clumsy Burnette, but they are so intent on their game that they hardly notice. This may have been fine for one of Columbia's "Three Stooges" shorts, but it had no place in a Western. Generally, Smiley was fun to watch, especially when his slapstick was under control.

The Starrett pictures were made with rural and small-town audiences in mind, and they were a far cry from the caliber of the movies Smiley had made with Gene Autry. Because of Autry's singing, his movies appealed to a much broader segment of the population.

Although Starrett did appreciate Smiley's hard work and his many personal appearances to promote the Durango features, Burnette was not his favorite sidekick. Starrett said several times he preferred the low-key humor of Cliff "Ukulele Ike" Edwards.

Almost three months after the Starrett series officially ended production, Smiley teamed with Autry for his final six films, all of which were 1953 Columbia releases.

It is ironic that Smiley and Gene wound up closing out their cinema

Smiley Burnett

& Vince Miles
AKA Doc Moody

careers together at Columbia since they had started together 18 years earlier at Republic. Prior to Smiley rejoining Gene at Columbia, Autry's sidekick had been Pat Buttram, but Buttram had been seriously injured during the filming of one of the Autry 1950 TV shows. Gene brought in Smiley as a replacement for Buttram in the 1951 Columbia feature WHIRLWIND. Including the Republic, and the last six Autry Columbia features, Smiley appeared in 57 pictures with Gene. *(Note: See the section titled PAT BUTTRAM AND THE CANNON.)*

SMILEY ENDS BIG SCREEN CAREER

Smiley left films in 1953, but was extremely popular at fairs, rodeos, and theaters. In fact, he led a life of nonstop touring and declared in the late 1950s that he had made more than 10,000 personal appearances up to that point.

In 1958, he was a guest performer, along with Tex Ritter and other stars, on the musical TV program "Ranch Party." The program ran for 39 episodes.

In 1962, Smiley donated his original movie hat and shirt to the Cowboy Hall of Fame in Oklahoma City, Oklahoma. He had five different hats, but the one he donated was the original hat and his favorite.

During Smiley's later years, he was a part-time resident of Springfield, Missouri. In Springfield, he taped a radio program for RadiOzark Enterprises, and frequently appeared on the television program, "Jubilee USA."

Smiley was back before the camera in 1963, this time in the CBS-TV country comedy series "Petticoat Junction." His hair was now mostly gray, and he was even heavier than before. Smiley was cast as "Charley Pratt," engineer of the Hooterville Cannonball train. His train partner was Rufe Davis, also a musician, and one-time Republic sidekick in *The Three Mesquiteers* films. Since Smiley's role was so small, many thought his talents were not fully utilized by those in charge of the program. During his work on "Petticoat Junction," he occasionally appeared in the companion series, "Green Acres."

In 1964, during a break in "Petticoat Junction," he traveled to Hawaii to take over as host for his friend Jimmie Dodd's "Aloha Club" TV series. Smiley and Dodd's friendships probably resulted because both were professing Christians. Strangely enough, Dodd, like Rufe Davis with whom Smiley worked on "Petticoat Junction," had also been member of *The Three Mesquiteers* series—and both played the same character, "Lullaby Joslin."

In 1965, Smiley had cataract surgery. At that time, the recuperation period was far longer than it is today. During his recovery, he kept busy writing songs.

About a year later, he began to feel weak and often out of breath. He was diagnosed with acute leukemia. Smiley, always the trouper, shared his illness with only his close relatives (not even with his old pal Gene Autry), and continued to work on "Petticoat Junction" until filming the last sequence of one of the programs. By then, he was so sick that an ambulance was called, and he was rushed to West Valley Hospital in Encino. He died one week later on February 16, 1967, at 9:05 p.m. He looked much older than his 55 years.

Gene Autry expressed sadness and surprise at Smiley's passing, but he did not attend his funeral. This puzzled many since he and Smiley had been good friends for over 30 years. Autry explained his reasoning for not attending: "Death, accidents, and illnesses are just difficult for me to handle. I won't attempt to explain that or defend it. Maybe it is related to a sense as to why I wanted my films to entertain the spirit, not challenge it. Why the endings were always happy and the plots often implausible. I felt that people saw enough unpleasantness in the normal turn of the wheel. I saw no need to force on them more of the hard reality that each of us comes to in our own time, in his own way."

Smiley's beloved wife Dallas passed away on February 19, 1976, at 5:00 a.m.

Who was Smiley Burnette? Perhaps Jon Guyot Smith, an expert on Gene Autry and Smiley, summed it up best in an issue of *Gene Autry's Friends*:

> He was a brilliant, self-taught entertainer, composer and musician. He was a gourmet chef and author of a cookbook. He was a thoroughly unaffected gentleman who frequently accepted dinner invitations from fans attending the local performances. He never smoked or drank, and he irritated Hollywood hostesses when he and Dallas requested water in lieu of wine at dinner parties. He was articulate and politically conservative, no doubt annoying New Deal-crazed cohorts at Republic Pictures. He was opposed to excessive permissiveness and lack of moral courage. He seemed incapable of recognizing the knavery of people he trusted. He loved to help others, and was loved virtually by everyone who worked with him ... Smiley Burnette brought much beauty, happiness and laughter into the world, making his mark and uplifting several generations of youngsters in his 55 years here ... through his films, music and recorded work, Smiley will be around longer than any of us can imagine.

This is certainly a fitting tribute to a man who established the trend for the movie cowboy sidekicks that followed him, and who became one of the best known personalities in the history of Western films.

SMILEY SPEAKS

Gene's worth $100 million dollars today. We went to his house for dinner once, but we didn't get much chance to talk. He had four phones going—all at the same time.

Gene will never know how grateful I am to him for all that he has done and if I told him, he would think I was gushy, so I don't tell him.

Gene Autry is the easiest person on the face of the earth to work with. Gene feels that if an actor steals the picture, it makes a good picture. All he wants is for the picture to be a Gene Autry picture. I never had a cross word with from him in all the years I worked with him, and I know at times I tried his patience.

(Pat Buttram, another Autry sidekick, issued a similar statement: "The picture MULE TRAIN (Columbia, 1950) shows you the character of Gene Autry, to let a guy come in and just take the whole part — it's my picture; it's the sidekick's picture for a change. Gene just encouraged it and helped out all he could to see that it held up as a picture rather than trying to hog it all for himself. A lot of guys in Westerns, if the sidekick happens to get a little ahead of the star on his horse — now this is no joke — the star would stop the scene and say, 'You get back; I want to be six feet ahead.' This was often the rule of a lot of them had, but Autry wasn't that way.")

(Smiley continues): I created that character (Frog), and I lived it. I never wanted to be an actor and to this day I don't consider myself one. I just played this one role. I never knew

Smiley Burnette looks happy with horse Black-Eyed Nellie now that Gene Autry has resumed filming with Republic for 1938's GOLD MINE IN THE SKY.

how to play anything else. There's really not much difference between Frog and "Charlie Pratt," the character I played on "Petticoat Junction."

My wife Dallas and I treat our marriage as a three-way deal. There's the part I like and she doesn't; the part she likes and I don't; and the part we both like. We don't have to do everything with each other.

Some folks worry about the cost of life without knowing the value of it. Way I figure it, happiness is like a butterfly. You can chase it, but if you just settle down it'll light on you.

I love everybody. It's nice to be important, but it's more important to be nice. The acid test of success is humility.

A reluctant Smiley Burnette appears to reject advice from Charles Starrett in an early 1950s *Durango Kid* entry.

A LETTER FROM SMILEY'S WIFE

Dear Friends:

Never let it be said that I put off writing letters because I dislike writing. Not only do I like to write, having earned my living for some years as a reporter, - but I met my husband that way.

As a reporter on the Hollywood Citizen-News, in June, 1935, I had written an article on Reb Russell, then a Western star in Hollywood, which had pleased his agent, Grace Causey.

So Grace gave a picnic supper in Fern Dell, one of Hollywood's loveliest sections of Griffith Park, and invited me as the guest of honor. Of course Reb was there, and with him came one Smiley Burnette, who had just a few months before arrived in Hollywood with Gene Autry to make pictures.

Smiley's merriment, his songs and accordion playing so entertained me that I counted the evening an exceptional success. Little did I realize that the spark of romance would be kindled from the friendship that began that night. It was not until the following summer, in 1936, that Smiley and I became engaged. We were married in October.

Not only did Smiley and I meet at a picnic but both of us always have been extremely fond of picnicking. We always keep a packed picnic basket in the trunk of each of our cars so we can picnic by the roadside whenever it suits us.

Always we have crackers, a jar of mayonnaise, a jar of cheese, cans of mixed vegetables and fruit and fruit juice with us. And after one experience of picnicking with the children at the beach last summer when I discovered I had forgotten a can opener and had to borrow one - I now carry one in the glove compartment and one in the trunk to make sure. If Smiley had been along, he would have thought of a way to rig up some kind of can and bottle opener. You just can't stump him, he is so resourceful.

Once when Smiley was on tour, he decided to cook some wieners for lunch by the roadside. He had a can of Sterno for heating but no Sterno stove on which to rest the pan. So he took a wire coat hanger and bent it into a shape that would hold the pan just above the can of heat. It made a fine stove!

Before closing I must tell you that Smiley has just made a new phonograph record for the Abbott label, "Mucho Gusto" and on the other side a song that Smiley wrote, "Highway 66." Even though I am prejudiced of course, I venture to say that either song has a good chance of becoming a hit and I'll warrant that Faber Robinson of Abbott Records agrees with me.

My very best to you all,

Dallas Burnette

If you don't find the record in your local music store in the near future, write to Smiley and tell him. You probably know the address, Box 100, Studio City, Calif.

FROG'S FRIENDS

Gene Autry: Smiley was an outstanding talent and a good friend. He was an important part of the success I had. I found him working on a little radio station during one of my early tours and brought him out to Hollywood with me. We sang many duets together. He worked in about 60 of my movies and accompanied me on most of my personal appearance tours. He was a sweet and easygoing fellow with a talent not everyone noticed behind that zany appearance. He could play more musical instruments than I knew existed—someone once said a hundred. He wrote 350 songs, and I never saw him take longer than an hour to compose one. But, best of all, he could make children laugh. He could talk to them as few entertainers—or parents could. I don't recall Smiley ever complaining. In fact, around a movie set, he was a human sunbeam. He had one of the softest hearts I ever knew. In that part of the Southwest where I was born, on the Texas-Oklahoma line, they had a saying to describe a man like Smiley who was so loyal: "He'll do to ride the river with." He and Pat Buttram were the best friends and sidekicks a cowboy could have. They both had big talents and big hearts.

Ann Rutherford *(She made four features with Smiley and Gene, and she was the first to get a screen kiss initiated by Gene):* Smiley was enormously talented. He was like a great, big huggy bear! This darling man ... he was gentle, dear, and he was a hugger—long before hugging was even fashionable.

I mean, before you ever knew what was happening, you were warmed to the cockles of your heart by a big, yummy hug from Smiley. He was always there to deliver his lines for your close-up. You know a lot of actors would go off and have a beer or something and let the script girl read it, but not Smiley. He was right there beside the camera. He was very inventive. Smiley was a dear man. He always came up to my mother and gave her a hug, and he made everybody feel good, and that's a wonderful gift.

Merle Travis *(singer, composer and instrumentalist):* Regarding his first meeting with Smiley, during a winter in Cincinnati, after Smiley had slipped and fallen on some ice: Smiley said to me, "I'd rather live in California and eat lettuce than live in Cincinnati and eat caviar." The next day I was on my way to California. That's the reason I went to Hollywood because of Smiley Burnette.

Mary Lee *(She worked in nine pictures with Autry and Burnette):* Smiley was very kind. He was particularly kind to me since I was so young. He was a sweet, adorable man who never used profanity.

Lupita Tovar *(She was in the Autry/Burnette 1939 Republic hit film, SOUTH OF THE BORDER):* Smiley was always nice.

Fay McKenzie *(She worked in five features with Autry and Burnette):* Smiley Burnette, like Gene, was wonderful. Actually, I had known Smiley earlier. We were in a George O'Brien picture, BORDER PATROLMAN.

Pierce Lyden: Smiley was a big man with a big heart. He did get kind of carried away with his comedy at times. I worked with him in some of Charlie Starrett's pictures. Smiley had been working in pictures for a long time and maybe it was hard to come up with new comedy routines, because I know, at times, Charlie was not too pleased with Smiley's antics. But Smiley was a nice man.

Gail Davis *(She appeared with Autry in 14 pictures — more than any other leading lady. She and Smiley worked together in five of these films):* He was the most lovable man who ever walked on the face of the earth ... just wonderful to work with, and I loved every minute we ever spent together.

Barbara Pepper *(She appeared in four movies with Smiley):* What a dear, warm-hearted man Smiley was. He worried a lot about how people seemed to be tearing at each other. He understood faith and love and helping one another. Bless him; violence was just not his nature. He loved people and animals and kids. Oh, how he loved the kids—not just for show or publicity. His kind of wholesome humor is rare nowadays. He didn't think it funny to get laughs by hurting others. I wish there were more Smiley Burnettes in the world today. It would be a happier place.

June Storey *(She made 10 features with Gene and Smiley):* Smiley was a tremendous person. Making Westerns was very hard and often hot and dirty work, and some days I would come in exhausted. Smiley would get a pan of cool water and wash and massage my feet. While I worked with Smiley, he and his wife arranged for the adoption of 39 other children. They had four children, and all were adopted. I think you can see that

Smiley was a humble person who cared deeply for children. Smiley had no jealousy, just a kind and wonderful man.

Dale Evans: Smiley was a wonderful Christian man. I just loved him.

Patsy Montana *(She worked with Smiley in the 1939 Republic film, COLORADO SUNSET):* I liked Smiley as a friend for many reasons. He was such a great help to me during my picture with Gene. He was wonderful to his parents, and was a prolific songwriter.

Pat Buttram: Smiley did more to help sidekicks in movies than anyone because he established it as part of the (Autry) series. He always said, "You know when the elevator gets near the top floor, send it down to bring up somebody else." He was always working with young kids. I think he was an inspiration to a lot of kids, and I loved the guy. I really understood him—maybe because I didn't have to ride alongside of him. He was always a friend of mine and a wonderful memory.

Oliver Drake *(director):* Smiley Burnette was one of the funniest men in the picture business and a nice guy. I got to know Smiley better than most people because we wrote music together.

Rufe Davis: Smiley, the person, was someone I was proud to know and be a friend of. He had an outlook on life that only a few people were able to master. As you probably know, he liked to help people who were sincere get ahead; he helped many people.

Curt Massey *(He sung the title song to "Petticoat Junction"):* Smiley was a wonderful man of great worth as well as talent ... and his life was well-lived and well-loved.

Hank Patterson *(Fred Ziffel in "Petticoat Junction"):* He was a clever man, had a splendid reputation, and was well-liked in his profession. He worked with me on "Green Acres" about two weeks before he died. On the set, I talked with him quite a bit, and I did not detect that he was ill at that time.

Lori Saunders *("Bobbie Jo Bradley" on CBS-TV's "Petticoat Junction"):* Smiley, as his name indicates, was always happy and always had a smile on his face. No one knew how ill he was, let alone the fact that he was ill at all. For Smiley was always fun to be with, whistling and rolling merrily along with

The cast from "Petticoat Junction." Standing: Rufe Davis, Smiley. Sitting: Bea Benaderet, Edgar Buchanan. On steps: Pat Woodall, Jeannine Riley, Linda Kaye.

life as if he owned it. I can recall many times on the set of "Petticoat Junction" how some of us would gather around and listen to his humorous stories and tales of past escapades. We, his friends and fans, are certainly going to miss Smiley Burnette, and always remember what a wonderful person he really was.

Don Kay "Little Brown Jug" Reynolds: I remember Smiley as a very talented, generous man. He was fun to be around. He made me laugh a lot.

Smiley on CBS-TV's "Petticoat Junction" (1963-67), his last acting assignment.

FROG FRICTION

At times, some of the actors who worked with the rotund comedian were not too thrilled with, or misunderstood, Burnette's attitude—among them were Charles Starrett, Slim Andrews and Sunset Carson. However, the positive remarks about Burnette far outweigh the negative ones.

Bob Livingston: I didn't want to work with Smiley. I didn't like Smiley's brand of humor. The guy personally? All right. Anything was all right (with me). I just couldn't picture that brand of humor working.

Pat Buttram: He did go his own way a lot.

Oliver Drake: I heard friends of Gene's, who were probably jealous of Smiley and who would have liked to take Smiley's place, trying to cause trouble (saying negative things about Burnette).

Jimmy Wakely: Sometimes distributors would tell Smiley Burnette that Gene couldn't make it without him … they were wrong. Even though Smiley was strong (in Autry's movies) and a very big part of the pictures, he wasn't 30 percent. You could take Smiley out and you still had the best series of Westerns … Smiley starred with Sunset Carson and Eddie Dew (also Bob Livingston), and it didn't happen; it didn't work.

Charles Starrett: They brought Smiley over to work in my pictures. I guess you could say we got off to a bad start. One day he told me he had been hired to give my pictures a shot in the arm. This did not set too well with me because I had been working for the studio for 10 years and my pictures had always done well at the box office. I think I got along with Smiley as well as any actor who worked with him. He was a

Dixie Ice Cream premium. This formal Republic photo of Smiley Burnette was probably taken during mid-late 1936.

Gene, Ann Rutherford and Smiley have a happy time together during COMIN' 'ROUND THE MOUNTAIN (Republic, 1936). Take notice of Burnette wearing an early "Frog" hat.

pretty aggressive guy to work with. I know there had been a little friction at times between Gene and Smiley.

Smiley was allowed free rein on his music in my films. I would usually just leave the set and wait until I got a call to come back. I liked Smiley, and I think he liked me. You must remember, too, he was active all the time between pictures. He would go out on the road and make personal appearances which only helped our pictures. He worked hard, and made a lot of personal appearances. He was an asset to my pictures.

Slim Andrews: I worked in a Gene Autry picture (COWBOY SERENADE, Republic, 1942) with Smiley and did a scene with him that I thought turned out real funny. A little later, Smiley said, "Hey Bud, you're not going to be in any more Autry pictures; I'm the comedian around here." I thought he was kidding, but he was serious. He knew what he was talking about because I never made any more Autry pictures.

Sunset Carson: When I started at Republic, they teamed me up with Smiley Burnette. Smiley was pretty cold to me in the first few pictures. I was awfully green and could have used his help at the time. I don't know if someone told him or not, but he kind of softened up around the last picture.

When we made FIREBRANDS OF ARIZONA, reception to the film was only mediocre. Back in that time people liked to see more serious action. Things like the wagon blowing up with old Tom London just sitting there with a guy next to him, and they just kept talking like nothing happened, weren't appreciated then.

The thing I remember most about Frog is that he was always eating. When they'd holler "Action!" or something, he'd have to have someone hold his ice cream or milkshake.

Jean Rouverol *(She worked with Gene Autry and Smiley in the 1938 movie, WESTERN JAMBOREE):* I was shooting a scene with Smiley Burnette. I couldn't understand how I always ended up with my back towards the camera. The cameraman called me over and said, "Don't let him (upstage you). Complain." So I did, aloud to everybody. I learned subsequently, Smiley did that to everybody he worked with. *Everybody!*"

FRUGAL FROG

Some of Smiley's acquaintances have criticized him, perhaps unfairly, over his various gimmicks to raise money. Smiley was not one to talk about his financial affairs—outside of his family. His troubles occurred when his unscrupulous business manager failed to pay many of Smiley's bills, which drove Smiley to verge of bankruptcy. To Smiley's credit, he was determined to do the honorable thing and pay off all he owed, and he had to work almost night and day to get his finances back in good order. Had those, making the following comments, known the truth about Smiley's plight, undoubtedly, they would have been more understanding and not have made some of the following statements:

Jock Mahoney: Smiley was a hell of a businessman. He was a tough guy with a buck. When he would go on tour, he would have a guy there with a camera. Smiley would have his picture taken with any kid in the audience. The kid would get a stub with a number of his picture, and Smiley would get a buck. When the picture was developed, it would be sent back to the kid. This was way back in the late 1940s when a buck was a buck.

(Later on, Smiley became one the first entertainers to take a Polaroid camera with him on personal appearance tours. He *would charge to have his photo taken with a fan, and then autograph it for the fan).*

Pee Wee King: *(King was probably referring to the above statement by Mahoney):* In the theaters, he always had a way to empty the house to bring another crowd in. Smiley'd say, "Okay little boys and girls, right after the stage show old Frog will be out behind the theater. If you come out there, you can have your picture made with Frog."

Pat Buttram: He was an enterprising guy; he had all kind of gimmicks going, but he helped a lot of people.

Kirby "Sky King" Grant: He was one the greediest persons I have ever known. You know that shirt that he wore, that black checkered shirt? He bought bolts of seconds of that material at Penney's. He cut off little inch squares and fastened them to a card with his autograph on it and sold it for two bits apiece. He would, of course, make a lot of friends around the country on his tours, and he would never, never, stay in a hotel or

Pee Wee King, Smiley and Carolina Cotton happily entertain.

motel; he would always go to these acquaintances and stay and live off them. If he could have sold his toenail parings, he probably would have.

Gene Autry: It so happens that Smiley Burnette is a very frugal man who doesn't believe allowing anything to waste. We had this scene, in one of my television shows, where it called for Sheila Ryan to pelt him with bag of tomatoes. That evening, when the set workers moved in to clean up the mess, they discovered someone had already scraped up the squashed tomatoes and made off with them. Knowing Smiley and his saving ways, we immediately suspected he was the guilty party. And sure enough, when Sheila went over to his trailer to check, there he was cooking up a fine tomato stew.

(The tomato-throwing incident Gene Autry was referring to between Smiley Burnette and Sheila Ryan actually happened within the first few minutes of Gene's PACK TRAIN (Columbia, 1953). Smiley never appeared in any of the Autry 30-minute CBS-TV shows released between 1950 and 1956.)

(Even his fan club publication, "The Westerner," was used to hawk items as it advertised "Genuine Indian relics at a special price" exclusively to Smiley Burnette Fan Club members.)

```
THIS COUPON ENTITLES THE BEARER TO ONE

          Complimentary
    SUNNY UP SUPER SNACK SANDWICH
                 AT THE
    SMILEY BURNETTE CHECKERED SHIRT
             SANDWICH SHOP

    _____ Mgr.
```

THEY'RE WRITING ABOUT SMILEY

Hans Wollstein (*All-Movie Guide*): As Autry became a major name in Hollywood, almost single-handedly establishing the long-lasting Singing Cowboy vogue, Burnette was right there next to him, first with Mascot and then, through a merger, with the newly formed Republic Pictures, where he remained through June 1944. The culmination of Burnette's popularity came in 1940, when he ranked second only to Autry in a *Box-office Magazine* popularity poll of Western stars, the lone sidekick among the Top Ten. Perhaps not everyone's cup of tea—his style of cute novelty songs and tubby slapstick humor could, on occasion, become quite grating. Burnette, nevertheless, put his very own spin on B-Westerns and became much imitated. In fact, by the 1940s, there were two major trends of sidekick comedy in B-Westerns: Burnette's style of slapstick prairie buffoonery, also practiced by the likes of Dub Taylor and Al St. John; and the more character-defined comedy of George "Gabby" Hayes, Andy Clyde, et al. Burnette refined his naïve, but self-important, Frog Millhouse character through the years at Republic Pictures—called "Frog," incidentally, from the way his vocals suddenly dropped into the lowest range possible. But the moniker belonged to the studio and he was plain Smiley Burnette thereafter. When Autry entered the service in 1942, Burnette supported Sunset Carson, Eddie Dew, and Bob Livingston, before switching to Columbia Pictures' *Durango Kid* series starring Charles Starrett. But despite appearing in a total of 56 Durango Westerns, Burnette was never able to achieve the kind of chemistry he had enjoyed with Autry, and it was only fitting that they should be reunited for the final six Western features Gene would make. Although his contribution to Autry's phenomenal success was sometimes questioned (minor cowboy star Jimmy Wakely opined that Autry had enough star power to have made it with any comic sidekick), Smiley Burnette remained extremely popular with young fans throughout his career, and although not universally beloved within the industry, he has gone down in history as the first truly popular B-Western comedy sidekick. Indeed, without his early success, there may never have been the demand for permanent sidekicks.

Don Miller (*Hollywood Corral*): Burnette had been with Autry on his radio show and entered films with him. For Burnette, it was the beginning of a new career as a Western clown. Burnette became so adept at his broad buffoonery that he contributed new directions to the course of comedy relief, and emphasized the advantage of the hero having a court jester. It (his comedy) overshadowed his genuine talent and facility for composing.

Jon Tuska (*The Filming of the West*): Regarding PHANTOM EMPIRE: Comedy was singularly confined to slapstick antics and simply incompetent and stupid behavior. (Smiley) placed more impediments in the hero's path than the villains could.

While humor had been in the Western almost from the beginning, and sidekicks had been around since the early 1920s, the Autry films introduced the "stooge" as a stock character.

Credit goes to Burnette probably as much as to Autry for making a stooge a regular feature of the Western melodrama for the next two decades. Countless imitators stepped forth, and nearly every cowboy in the forties had at least one stooge, some of them two or more.

When Smiley started at Republic with Autry, Gene put him under a personal contract. It meant all of Smiley's songs belonged to Gene, and Gene started a music publishing company. Then Gene went into the Air Force, and Smiley's contract ran out, and he could go to Columbia. By 1950, Smiley was darned near destitute except for the money he got for the Starrett Westerns. He went to Gene and said, "Listen, can I have some royalties on my songs?" Gene said, "No, they belong to me. But I will do this for you, I'll let you star in my last series at Columbia." With him it was all business, and the Autry films were primarily means of income and not his greatest income.

Merrill McCord (*Brothers of the West — The Lives and Films of Robert Livingston and Jack Randall*): Without his benefactor Autry, Burnette was a little like the proverbial fish out of the water; and Republic appeared unsure what to do with him. Burnette was put into four films with Rogers, two with Dew, the three with Livingston, and four with Sunset Carson before he would go to Columbia in May 1945 to work with Charles Starrett. However, with these other cowboy players, Burnette never achieved the screen chemistry he had with Autry. When Burnette worked with Livingston, his salary was about $1,000 a week, far greater than Livingston's.

Douglas B. Green (*Singing In the Saddle*): Although Burnette is best remembered as an accomplished accordion player, he played almost anything that he could be plucked, tooted, honked, squeezed or fingered. In addition to his movies, he later had his own Mutual network radio show (with musical support by the Whippoorwills) and was the first supporting actor to appear regularly on the yearly top ten moneymaking Western stars. Burnette was a compulsive songwriter, and while the majority of his songs were forgettable, novelties such as "Minnie the Moocher at the Morgue," his "Ridin' Down the Canyon"—written in Gene Autry's Buick on their first exploratory trip to Hollywood—remain in the pantheon of all-time Western classics.

Jon Guyot Smith (article in *Gene Autry's Friends*): His contract with Columbia stipulated that he would be paid for the Starretts if and when they reached the small screen, but a plan to release them for TV in 1957 was aborted. Dismayed, Smiley approached Columbia with an offer to buy the television rights to *The Durango Kid* series. They said he could buy them ten at a time for $10,000 per title—but he would have to start with the *earliest* films in the Starrett series, made years before Smiley even appeared in them! Needless to say, he declined the offer.

There were four issues of Smiley's comic books during the 1950 months of March, May, July, and October distributed by Fawcett.

The front and back of Smiley comic #3 (July 1950). Burnette also had individual monthly stories in "Six Gun Heroes" comics at this same time.

Columbia announced a 1954-55 series to star Jack (aka Jacques) Mahoney and Smiley, the first of which was to be PANHANDLE TERRITORY. This series was never made, although Mahoney later told an interviewer he definitely recalled making PANHANDLE TERRITORY with Smiley, and he enjoyed the experience.

Eric Hoffman (article in *Favorite Westerns*): Opinions have been divided upon Burnette's contributions to the quality of the series (Durango Kid) ... or the amount and quality of the comedy element, period ... especially with the number of entries per year. It would often be obvious that the material of his character was being stretched a mite thin. Besides his acting duties, Burnette, periodically, would come up with one or two specialty songs for himself to perform in nearly every one of the Starrett films he appeared in.

Dorothy Kort Jadlowiec (from the Arabella and Company website): I met Smiley Burnette many years ago on a bitter cold day in Pittsburgh. I was 16, and getting autographs of my favorite stars was my passion. He was appearing in the stage show of a downtown theater, and I was one of three eager but freezing teenagers standing outside the stage door. When the door suddenly opened and one of the stagehands appeared, we were prepared to run (stagehands didn't approve of autograph hounds), but he beckoned for us to come inside. Astonishment turned to awe when Smiley not only greeted us graciously, but ordered up a round of hot chocolates to warm us up. He talked and told stories about his life in Hollywood while we sipped our toddies, gave us the autographs and then firmly ordered us to go home out of the cold. I never forgot that warm, friendly man. Wherever you are, Smiley, you are still in my thoughts.

Bruce Hickey (article in *Wrangler's Roost*): The fact that archetypal buffoon Smiley Burnette achieved popularity (if the polls are to believed) in the B-Western era is hard to understand looking back from this point of time. Viewing the Autrys and the Starretts as a kid in the 1940s, he was hard to endure even back then, and his solo time on the screen was the time to head for the popcorn or ice cream counter. It is interesting to note that Gene Autry never allowed him the "over the top" antics he displayed in the Charles Starrett Westerns. Thankfully, in this video and DVD age, we have remote control and it's possible to fast forward through his buffoonery.

WESTERN FILM FANS SPEAK

I have asked several friends, who are also knowledgeable Western fans, to contribute their thoughts about Smiley. Since comedy is a personal thing, it is not surprising that there were positive, as well as negative comments, regarding Smiley's performances.

Bill Russell (author): I think Smiley contributed greatly to the B-Western. And I think his best work was with Autry. A highly talented musician, writer and player, I personally did not care for his antics as a sidekick. I thought there was always a little too much of him; in other words, I could take him for a while but after that, goodbye Frog. One of his best lines ever delivered came in, I believe, RED RIVER VALLEY (I may be wrong here), when he and Gene are forced to plunge off a cliff into the water while being chased by an outlaw gang. As they are struggling from the water on the other shore, Smiley is being pulled out holding onto his horse's tail and saying to Gene, "I always wondered what a horse's tail was for." He may also have been an important ingredient to Gene's success. Gabby Hayes, on the other hand, was funny and cranky, and I personally liked him better. I never grew tired of Hayes on the screen.

Larry Welch (fan): When I was 10 years old, I thought Smiley was the funniest sidekick alive. I even picked my on-line name after him "KanSmiley." But now that I am a few years older, I know he worked well with Gene, but forget it with the Durango Kid.

Les Adams (author): I first encountered Smiley when I was six years old. I thought he was funnier than all get-out, especially when he would change his voice. By the time, in 1944, when he was in the first four Sunset Carson films, I could barely tolerate him...and couldn't tolerate him at all when he showed up in *The Durango Kid* films. Personally, I would have preferred that Columbia had kept Dub Taylor in those films, strictly as the lesser of the two evils in my pre-teen mind. Sixty years later, I haven't changed my mind about that. Smiley was a vastly-talented man music-wise, when he wasn't knocking off some ditty in ten minutes to fit a plot device. I still walk around humming his "It's My Lazy Day." But that's probably because, for some unknown reason, that is one of the few songs ever written that I can hum (and even sing) on key.

Hans Wollstein (author): Truth be told, I've never been overly fond of Smiley Burnette. All the comedic sidekicks are matters of taste and temperament, and although I can easily tolerate "Gabby" Hayes or Andy Clyde character actors playing a role, I have a hard time with the prairie clowns: Burnette, Dub Taylor, and Al St. John. To me, it's just so much shtick. Burlesque routines that tend to become action stoppers. In Smiley's case, the nadir remains his appearance in some of the early Republic serials where his particular brand of humor completely clashed with the rhythm of the plots. But I do like Burnette's songwriting. I find him a highly inventive composer and lyricist, and his musical interludes in the Gene Autrys are usually most enjoyable. He is at his best with Autry, their easy camaraderie is obvious—but you can almost feel that his presence in the Charles Starretts was not entirely welcome by Starrett himself.

Ken Jones (author): I imagine as a kid I probably liked him, but can't really remember. I believe I even saw him on the stage once. As an adult, I really do not care for him, and I certainly have no favorite role unless it is his role as the engineer on "Petticoat Junction." He seemed more sensible there. In spite of all his musical talents — and they were aplenty — I just do not like his brand of comedy and even though I watch a few old Westerns on television, I will not watch one with him in it. I guess that just about sums it up for Smiley.

Jim Kocher (a fan who has attended many film festivals): He may have been the most talented of all the B-Western sidekicks. He was superb as a Western music writer, singer and instrumentalist. What instrument could he not play? Don't forget, he wrote much of the music in untold B-Westerns. Smiley is arguably the best comedic sidekick to grace the silver screen. He appeared with Gene Autry, Roy Rogers, Charles Starrett and many others. He also worked in radio and, in later years, in television. The world was a much happier place while he was in it.

Doug Morris (newspaper publisher): Those B-Western cowboy movies we loved so well growing up seemed to be like a Betty Crocker cake mix — put in an action hero, a comic sidekick, music, and stir until the bad guys cried uncle. When Gene Autry loaded up and headed for Hollywood, he also took along humor, and music, in the person of Smiley Burnette. The rest, as they say, is history. Smiley's contributions, mostly through his music, his comedy, ring-eyed Nellie, and the chemistry between him and Gene Autry certainly added up to much of the reason the duo became such a success in their early careers on the silver screen and in personal appearances.

Smiley is one in a long line of sidekicks such as George "Gabby" Hayes, Al "Fuzzy" St. John, Pat Brady and others. Though his comedy compared with the antics of Gabby and Fuzzy may be lacking, considering the whole package of humor and music, Smiley, arguably, may have been more talented and contributed as much as any of the others. Depends upon what makes you laugh, and Fuzzy St. John's humor always just kind of sneaked up on you while he thought no one was looking.

Gene Autry was always my favorite cowboy and, thus, Smiley became a favorite as his early sidekick. I always loved *The Durango Kid* series and Smiley got to perform many of his own songs, though he, and many complain, may have gotten in Starrett's way in those roles. Smiley was talented, said to have mastered more than 100 instruments, and wrote hundreds of songs — among them "Mama Don't Allow No Music Played in Here" and the classic "Ridin' Down the Canyon." He created the character "Frog Millhouse." However, He focused his musical attention on many children with songs like "God Loves Tennessee."

In the mid to late 1940s, he was Starrett's sidekick and billed as "The West's No. 1 Comic." The popularity of Gabby Hayes quite possibility could have won that title in a run-off election.

His strength was music and along with humor all rolled up in a checked shirt, a tattered black hat with a turned up brim, his character was infectious. His gangly walk, or run, evoked a smile, if not a belly laugh, as he was discovering or running away from trouble. He had his shortcomings—we all do—but most of my long-lasting memories of Smiley Burnette came from my childhood and are good, humorous, musical, and real. Perhaps he could have been making more movies instead of cooking and fishing. We should all have such shortcomings.

Somewhere, Gene and Smiley, and Roy, and Charles Starrett are riders in the sky ... until they bed down at night —that's when we look up and see stars!

Clint Mitchell (a fan): Smiley was probably the No. 1 comic sidekick in Westerns. My personal favorite was Gabby Hayes. I think of Smiley mostly for his work as the Durango Kid's sidekick, although I do remember him with Gene Autry and Sunset Carson.

Without Smiley, there would have been a giant vacuum in Westerns. He was a musical genius, but that never came across to a kid's mind. Yes, he could sing and play dozens of instruments and make you laugh, but I liked his acting, too. You know I cannot think of a single title of one of his Westerns I liked better than another. He has a star on the Hollywood Walk of Fame along with many of the other greats. So I view him as a positive contribution to the B-Western genre. What would the "lighter" side of these movies be without sidekicks like Smiley Burnette?

Paul Dellinger (author): Smiley obviously contributed to the B-Western to the point where his image is about as indelible as Gabby's. (His image was even taken off in the modern 1985 spoof RUSTLERS' RHAPSODY.) And he is indelibly linked to many of the Gene Autry movies, which have their place in movie history. I have to say that to me, personally, much of his comedy was too broad for my tastes.

I first encountered him in the Durango series and couldn't wait for the focus to get back to Charles Starrett, either as Steve or Durango. I had the same reaction to Dub "Cannonball" Taylor. I preferred the (usually) competent sidekicks such as Gabby, Fuzzy St. John, Raymond Hatton et al. I liked Smiley in small doses, but, as stated above, his thunder-blunder style of humor didn't appeal to me all that much, and while I know he was a multi-talented musician, neither did his singing. On those rare occasions where his screen character would come through in a crisis, he had me, but mostly he was the kind of sidekick who hindered more than helped the hero. Smiley always played Smiley (or Frog, which was the same thing), and none of his roles stand out in my mind more than another. They all seemed about the same. Perhaps I'd have to pick his dual role as Smiley and outlaw Beefsteak Discoe in the comedy, FIREBRANDS OF ARIZONA (Republic, 1944).

Bill Sasser (Williamsburg film promoter): Smiley Burnette lasted a long time and was voted in the top-ten Western stars, but I never was a big fan. I did not enjoy his humor. The movies with Sunset Carson, where he talked to the audience, were absurd, even for kids. He did not help the Durangos. In fact, he diminished them. I have no favorite Smiley movies.

Ross Pittman (a fan): I was working for the television station in Lake Charles, Louisiana, (KPLC-TV) in the late 1950s, and Smiley was appearing at a rodeo in a town near there. Smiley and the rodeo promoter came over and did an on-the-air promotion. It was a brief visit, but I can say he was a very nice, congenial person. Had his black hat and polka-dot shirt, shook hands with everyone, and was on his way. He was just "Frog."

Grady Franklin (former publisher of *The Western Film*): No doubt about it, Smiley Burnette was an outstanding talent. Perhaps a lot of his entertainment abilities were squandered on being just plain silly.

Maybe I didn't like that side of his personality because I was a dirt poor East Tennessee kid and had little appreciation of such antics at the time. The time, in fact, was my youth and a period known as the Great Depression. Having food on the table, shoes on the feet, and a warm house in winter were more important to a young boy than a few laughs with Smiley at the Ritz Theater on Saturday. Granted, Westerns did serve as a momentary escape from the hardships of that depressed time in our nation's history.

At the time, I thought more of Tex Ritter's sidekick Slim Andrews than the likes of Smiley or Syd Saylor and especially that silly clown with Don "Red" Barry. Let's see, what was his name? Oh, Wally Vernon. Yuuuuuk!! Another sidekick who gets that same rating from Old Grady is the guy with James Warren in SUNSET PASS (RKO, 1946) and CODE OF THE WEST (RKO, 1947). The name: John Laurenz. He was just awful in comparison to the "Chito Rafferty" of Richard Martin. I suppose I liked sidekicks who helped the star instead of comic pals or just plain idiot sidekicks.

Fuzzy Q. Jones was OK. I liked him better in the early Westerns when he was razor thin. Remember him with George Houston in FRONTIER SCOUT (Grand National, 1938)? He was a sidekick to Wild Bill Hickok in a Civil War Western. All that is in comparison to his later days with Lash LaRue when he tended to repeat himself. And Dub Taylor was OK by me although some could not stand his deep South accent. He was even more enjoyable in his later film work and as a guest at festivals. But a really great sidekick, in my opinion, was Ray Whitley. He had authentic Western musical talent, he could deliver his lines, and he would help Tim Holt when needed.

Now, Smiley had some of those fine attributes, but he carried silly to the extreme. Smiley could play just about any musical instrument. He learned to do that in his native Illinois where, in that toddling town of Chicago, he performed on WLS Radio's National Barn Dance. He answered a call from Gene Autry and did his best work with the great singing cowboy.

Sure, Smiley worked with *The Durango Kid*, Bob Livingston and Sunset Carson in shoot-em-ups at Republic. But his best days seemed to be with Autry.

Throughout his career, Smiley was able to show off his ability with all those instruments and showcase many of the numerous songs he wrote. Just a great talent!

But, unfortunately, not my ideal kind of sidekick. Rest in peace Smiley, along with that other Illinois guy Cal Shrum, and the likes of Slim Andrews, Max Terhune, Fuzzy Q. Jones (and I do know that the name is Al St. John).

Oh, one final thought: seeing these guys in person makes them grow on you. I never met Smiley, for instance. But I have enjoyed the company of Slim Andrews, Richard Martin, Dub

Taylor and Fuzzy Q. Jones' lord and master, Lash LaRue. My appreciation of them is greater because of those moments together. Now don't get me wrong. As much as I like these guys, I'm in no real hurry to see them again face to face.

Billy Weathersby (a fan): In the early fifties, Smiley came to town to perform at the local school. I was selected to help him load and unload his trunk. I remember how cluttered and crowded the whole car was. He didn't talk or smile, just told me what to do. After the show, he gave me a signed picture and he drew a frog on it. He just signed "frog" on the other autographs, still without smiling or recognizing the person across from him. But make no mistake, he put on a great show and the crowd was very entertained. I thought Smiley was great in BOOTS AND SADDLES (Republic, 1937) with Autry, and in SMOKY CANYON (Columbia, 1952) with Charles Starrett.

Boyd Magers (Western film historian/publisher): The meeting and historic pairing of Gene Autry and Smiley Burnette is widely known, and I'm sure retold elsewhere in this book. Gene and Smiley's friendship was based on common struggles, mutual respect, similar interests and the genuine nature of both men.

Fate, persistence and Lady Luck all had a share in their success. In 1942, When Gene entered the service during WWII, Republic cast Smiley in several Roy Rogers pictures, along with those of Eddie Dew. Dew's *John Paul Revere* series quickly flopped. At Smiley's urging, Republic decided to try a new tack by top-billing comic Smiley Burnette over their new leading man, Oklahoma/Texas rodeo cowboy Michael Harrison whom Republic prexy Herbert J. Yates promptly christened Sonny "Sunset" Carson. (The Sonny was dismissed after this first film.) Smiley received top billing over the fledgling star in the first four films, a first in B-Western history.

Republic originally intended to do eight with "Frog" in the "lead," but the fan mail for Sunset was so overwhelming Republic decided to let Sunset go on his own. What transpired between Yates and Burnette's ego at this time is unknown, but after 10 years at the studio, Smiley took a hike. Off the screen altogether in 1945, he re-emerged with Charles Starrett at Columbia in 1946. With a sidekick technically in the lead, Republic began another gimmick with CALL OF THE ROCKIES in which the kids in the theatre audience were asked to participate in the on-screen action. In this one, as a "badman" chases Sunset and Frog at the end of the picture, Smiley turns to the audience and asks them all to go "Bang," apparently "shooting" the outlaw off his horse. The quite unusual final denouement in CODE OF THE PRAIRIE brings the audience into the explanation of the picture as Smiley turns directly to the audience and says, "You kids go home now. You been in here all day."

Smiley and Sunset's best was FIREBRANDS OF ARIZONA, a B-Western classic! The funniest film Republic ever made. Determined to cure her hypochondriac, pill-guzzling, ranch hand Smiley (Frog) Burnette, ranch owner Peggy Stewart sends Frog off to a distant medical specialist, accompanied by his pal Sunset. Frog and Sunset are fired upon by a posse believing Frog to be wanted outlaw Beefsteak Discoe, whom he resembles to a T. Badmen, also believing Frog to be their boss Beefsteak, rescue the pair who hightail it into town where the local populace, including horses and cigar store Indians, run from them in terror—again mistaking Frog for Beefsteak. Sheriff Earle Hodgins (who practically steals the picture with his mannerisms and ad-libs) captures Frog, pegging him as the notorious outlaw. Poor Frog is about to be hung (at this point every "hanging joke" ever conceived is trotted out) until the real outlaw pulls a stage robbery. Then it's a merry who's who mix-up comedy of errors of which there is none funnier. The surrealistic scenes between Frog and wagon driver Tom London are absolutely delightful. Nothing like FIREBRANDS OF ARIZONA has ever been seen in B-Westerns before or since. This was Smiley's last of four with Sunset who was getting the build-up from Republic.

Smiley left Republic to join Charles Starrett at Columbia, and Carson went on to unparalleled B-Western popularity, only to unfortunately self-destruct in less than three years.

Admittedly, I was never a big fan of Smiley Burnette, although I recognize how important he was to the success of Gene Autry's Republic Westerns. Therefore, in my "Top 100 Cowboys of the Century" special edition of *Western Clippings*, I ranked him the #2 sidekick behind George "Gabby" Hayes. When Gene entered the service, Republic didn't quite know what to do with Burnette.

Smiley's Westerns at Columbia with Charles Starrett are like night and day to his pictures opposite Autry. Watching a Durango Kid with Smiley you'll notice the story and action usually come to a screeching halt while Smiley "does his thing." Only rarely were the scriptwriters able to truly fold Smiley's antics into the storyline. When Smiley rejoined Gene at Columbia it added a nostalgic charm missing in other Autry

Don't shoot, Smiley. You've got to help Gene Autry finish filming on **GOLD MINE IN THE SKY (Republic, 1938).**

Columbias. Gene seemed positively enlightened by the return of his old friend, most noticeable when the pair, in a simple scene, is riding together on a wagon dueting on "Tweedle-O-Twill." Pat Buttram once observed, "There's always a party going on inside Smiley."

Smiley, when not clowning. Here, more relaxed.

FROG'S FAN CLUB

Like some other B-Western performers, Smiley had his own fan club — created by Smiley himself. Some of the cowboy heroes had fan clubs, but apparently Smiley was the only sidekick to have one. It seems the club was a self-promotional idea by Smiley since members were to pledge to see all of his pictures, tell others where to see them, and to write letters each month to the studio about Smiley.

> *Listed below are the cardinal pledges of the Smiley Burnette Fan Club. We hope every one of you will read them and remember their importance, for they constitute the club's basic foundation:*
>
> *I promise to make every effort to see Smiley "Frog" Burnette in every picture he is in.*
> *I promise always to let my friends know where and when they can see "Frog" in pictures.*
> *I promise to show my loyalty to "Frog" by writing him once each month faithfully and will offer constructive and helpful suggestions regarding his pictures.*
> *I promise to show my interest in our club by doing everything I can to get new members.*
> *I promise to carry my membership card with me at all times and to obey the pledges guiding my club.*

(It is doubtful many of the youngsters knew the meaning of some of the words used in the Fan Club card pledges, such as "cardinal," "constitute," "foundation," and "constructive.")

"Now, Tadpole, watch out for women. They're up to no good."

With Smiley setting type, you can bet something will go wrong for him in WINNING OF THE WEST (Columbia, 1953).

Smiley and Durango have spotted trouble from one of their late 1940s B-Westerns for Columbia Pictures.

"There he is, Sunset. Go get him," Burnette says to Carson while filming at Republic Pictures in 1944.

Burnette takes a well-deserved breather after pulling the rickshaw with Kay Hughes and Gene Autry in THE BIG SHOW (Republic, 1936). Actually, this was a posed shot.

SMILEY THE SONGSTER
Thanks in part to Larry Hopper

Among artists who have recorded Burnette songs are: Gene Autry, Cass County Boys, Daughters of the Purple Sage, Eddie Dean and The Plainsmen, Don Edwards, Shirley Field, Scotty Harrel, The Jimmy Wakely Trio, Tem Martin with Cliffie's Stonehead Band, Vaughn Monroe, Rich O'Brien, Roy Rogers and Sons of the Pioneers, Sons of the Pioneers, Stafford Sisters (Jo on lead), Merle Travis, Zeb Turner, Ozie Waters and The Plainsmen, Willis Brothers, and Smiley himself.

There are at least 212 different performances in films of songs written (or co-written) by Smiley. Of that number, five songs were used in two different films; six songs were used in three different films; and one song was used in four different films. Most of his songs were novelty items to fit the script of a particular film or for comedy relief.

He did write several classic songs (with co-credits): "Ridin' Down the Canyon" (Autry); "On the Strings of My Lonely Guitar" (Jimmy Wakely); "It's My Lazy Day," "End of the Trail," and "Mama Don't Like Music" (Autry).

Since Gene could neither read nor write music, and learned his songs from listening to performances, records or demo disks, you can be sure the credits were business deals since he had Smiley under personal contract. Gene's contribution on many of the songs credited to him is minimal.

In 1971, Burnette was inducted posthumously into the Nashville Songwriters Hall of Fame. The Hall also includes such B-Western performers as Jimmy Wakely, Gene Autry, Ray Whitley, Tex Ritter, and Bob Nolan.

On November 5, 1998, Smiley was inducted into the Western Music Association's Hall of Fame. Jackie Autry wrote a letter for the occasion:

> *Gene admired, respected and loved Smiley very much. He considered him a remarkably talented songwriter, musician and all around entertainer ... a cherished friend.*

(Western music critic O. J. Sikes provided the write-up for Smiley's induction):

> *Illinois native SMILEY BURNETTE (1911-1967) had never set foot in the West when he wrote his first cowboy song, "The Round-up in Cheyenne," for his friend Gene Autry to record in 1934. Some months later, deeply moved while driving through Arizona and New Mexico en route to Los Angeles, and seeing the splendor of the American West first-hand, Smiley wrote "Ridin' Down the Canyon" on the back of a magazine and sold it to Gene for five dollars.*

> *Smiley, who became the first musical sidekick in Western movies, composed nearly all of the songs for the early Gene Autry movies. These include "Wagon Train" (from THE SINGING VAGABOND), "The Old Covered Wagon" and "Someday in Wyoming" (from IN OLD SANTA FE), the moving "End of the Trail" (from SAGEBRUSH TROUBADOUR), "Let's Go Roaming Around the Range" (from THE OLD BARN DANCE) and "Hold On, Little Dogies, Hold On" (from*

MELODY TRAIL). Other outstanding Smiley Burnette compositions include "On the Strings of My Lonesome Guitar" (which was Jimmy Wakely's theme song in the 1940s), "Fetch Me Down My Trusty .45," "Ridin' All Day," "It's Indian Summer" and "I'll Go Ridin' Down That Old Texas Trail."

By that time the popularity polls indicated that Smiley Burnette had become one of the highest rated cowboy film stars in the Golden Era of the B-Western film; he was in such demand for his comedy as a sidekick to Gene Autry, Roy Rogers, Sunset Carson and Charles Starrett (the Durango Kid), that he no longer had the time needed to devote to composing. Many people tended to forget about his musical abilities, although he continued to play dozens of musical instruments on screen, on radio and in personal appearances. Nevertheless, his contribution to Western music is unquestionable. One WMA historian commented recently, "Smiley would deserve election to the Hall of Fame on the merits of 'Ridin' Down the Canyon,' alone." Of course, he did much more. As Pee Wee King said in a 1982 interview, "Smiley had the spirit of the West in him. That came out in the wonderful Western music he wrote."

Most of the songs listed here were written solely by Smiley. And many of his songs were used in more than one film. It is estimated this list contains 98% of Burnette's songs. This may be the first attempt by anyone to catalog Smiley's many songs.

Listed in alphabetical order

A-ROOTIE TOOT, A-ROOTIE TOOT
AIN'T LIFE SWELL
ALL NICE PEOPLE
AROUND THE CLOCK
AS OUR PALS RIDE BY
AS TIME GOES BY
BATHTUB KING, THE
BLACK, BLACK JACK OF ALL TRADES
BLUE LITTLE GIRL, A
CAN'T CRY FOR LAUGHING
CATFISH TAKE A LOOK AT THAT WORM
CAVE MAN SONG
CECIL COULD SEE WHAT HE WANTED TO SEE
CHIEF POCATELLO FROM THE CHEROKEES
CORNFED AND RUSTY (ANTIQUE AND DUSTY)
COW MILKING SONG
COWBOY MEDICINE SHOW, THE

COWBOY SHINDIG	DISH RAG BLUES
COWBOY'S LIFE, A	DIXIE INSTRUMENTAL SUITE
COWBOYS DON'T MILK COWS	DOCTOR MILLHOUSE
COYOTE CHORUS	DON'T BE MAD AT ME
CRAZY JUST LIKE ME	DON'T TRUST A BICYCLE RACER
CRICKET SONG, THE	DON'T WANT NOTHIN' — JUST LOOKIN'
DAY DREAM LARIAT	DONKEY ENGINE
DEAR OLD WESTERN SKIES	DOWN IN SLUMBERLAND
DENTIST SONG	DRIFTING SMOKE

DUSTY ROADS
ELMER, THE ABSENT MINDED COWBOY
END OF THE TRAIL, THE
ETIQUETTE BLUES
EVER LOVIN' MARSHAL
EXTRA, EXTRA (READ ALL ABOUT IT)
FAREWELL FRIENDS OF THE PRAIRIE
FAT CABALLERO, THE
FETCH ME DOWN MY TRUSTY .45
FICKLE FINGER OF FATE
FIDDLIN' FOOL
FIFE, THE
FIRE OF '41, THE
FIREMAN'S DAUGHTER, THE
FIVE MINUTES LATE AND A DOLLAR SHORT
FLOATIN' DOWN THE DEEP RIVER
FROG TUPLETTES (FROG SONG, THE)
FROM THE INDIES TO THE ANDES IN HIS UNDIES
GETTIN' SOME SLEEP
GOTTA GET A HORSE
GRANDPA FROG
GRASSHOPPER POLKA, THE
GREAT BURNETTE FROM CHIHUAHUA
GREAT GRANDDAD
GUIDE ME WESTERN STAR
HAPPY COBBLER, THE
HARMONICA BILL
HE DON'T LIKE WORK
HE WAS AN AMATEUR ONCE
HIKE YAA, MOVE ALONG
HOLD ON LITTLE DOGIES, HOLD ON
HOMINY GRITS
HONEY BRINGIN' HONEY TO YOU
HORSE-FEATHERS YODEL
HORSES AND WOMEN
HUNTIN' TROUBLE
HURDY GURDY MAN
HURRAY (WE'VE GOT A DATE WITH NOLAN)
I AIN'T GONNA DO TOMORROW
I CAN WHIP ANY MAN BUT POPEYE
I GOT THE SILLIES
I KEEP GOIN'
I KIN DANCE
I NEED A WORER-ER
I SAW HER FIRST
I SHOULD SAY
I THREW AWAY THE KEY TO HEAVEN
I WAS THAR
I WISH I'D SAID THAT
I WOULD HAVE BEEN DIFFERENT
I'D LOVE A HOME IN THE MOUNTAINS
I'D LOVE TO WED (ON THE PRAIRIE)
I'D MAKE A HIT WITH YOU
IF I WERE THE BOSS
IF YOU WANT TO BE HAPPY
I'LL BE GLAD TO SEE YOU
I'LL GO RIDING DOWN THAT OLD TEXAS TRAIL
I'M A COWBOY AND HOW BOY
I'M A TUMBLEWEED TENOR (WITH A BARITONE SOUL)
I'M GETTIN' A MOON'S EYE VIEW OF THE WORLD
I'M HUNTING A MOUNTAIN BALLAD
I'M JUST A LITTLE COWBOY
I'M DOOMED TO FOLLOW THE BUGLE
I'M TELLING MYSELF I AIN'T AFRAID
I'M OSCAR, I'M PETE
I'M TOO SMART FOR THAT
IN A CABIN ON A CLIFF IN CLEVELAND
IN MY LITTLE OLD HOUSE
IN MY VINE COVERED CABIN IN THE VALLEY
IT AIN'T MUCH HELP
IT ALL GOES TO SHOW YA
IT CAN'T BE AS BAD AS THAT
IT WAS JUST IN FUN
IT'S A HEAVENLY NIGHT OUT WEST
IT'S GOTTA GET BETTER BEFORE IT GETS WORSE
IT'S INDIAN SUMMER
IT'S MY LAZY DAY
IT'S MY TURN
IT'S THE LAW
I'VE GOT FINE RELATIONS
JUST COME ON IN
JUST IMAGINE THAT
KEEP GOIN' LITTLE PONY
KEEP IT IN THE FAMILY
KEEP YOUR EYE ON A SHOOTING STAR
KING OF PAIN
KITTY LOVED THE CALLIOPE
LAW AND ORDER
LAZY DAILY DOZEN
LET ME SLEEP
LET'S MAKE A DEAL
LET'S GO ROAMING AROUND THE RANGE
LI'L INDIAN
LITTLE MUD HOUSE
LIVE TO EAT
LONE COWBOY ON A LONE PRAIRIE, A
LOOKIN' POOR, FEELIN' RICH

LOST CHORD (LOOKING FOR THE)	MODERN DESIGN
LOUD AND FAST, FLOATIN' DOWN THE DEEP, DEEP RIVER	MORE WE GET TOGETHER, THE
LOUISVILLE LADY	MOTHER, HERE'S A BOUQUET FOR YOU
MAIL ORDER MUSIC	MY HOME TOWN
MAMA DON'T ALLOW MUSIC	MY JACKASS-O-PHONE
MAN IN THE MOON IS A COWBOY, THE	MY NEIGHBOR HATES MUSIC
MESS SONG	MY ORCHESTRA'S DRIVING ME CRAZY
MINNEHAHA (SHE GAVE THEM ALL THE HA HA)	MY PINTO PONY AND I
MINNIE THE MOOCHER AT THE MORGUE	MY PRAYER FOR TONIGHT
	NEVER SAY 'LOVE YOU' ON A POSTCARD
	NEW TEN GALLON HAT, A

Smiley's first song book, published in 1937.

NIGHT ON THE DESERT
NINETY NINE BULLFROGS
NO NEED TO WORRY
NOBODY FIRES THE BOSS
OH, WOE IS ME
OLD TEN GALLON HAT, THE
OLD COVERED WAGON, THE
ON MY WAY BACK HOME
ON THE MELODY TRAIL
ON THE STRINGS OF MY LONESOME
  GUITAR
OUR WHOLE FAMILY'S SMART
PAINTED DESERT
PART TIME SWEETHEART
PARADE SONG
PEDRO ENCHILADA
PEG LEG BANDIT
PRAIRIE DOG LAMENT, THE
PUSSY FOOT
RAINBOW TRAIL
RAINBOW VALLEY
RAISIN' RABBITS
RAMBLIN' BLOOD IN MY VEINS
RED RIVER SWEETHEART
RICH GET RICHER, THE
RIDIN' DOWN THE CANYON
RIDING ALL DAY
RING THE BELL
SAIL THE SEVEN SEAS
SCAREDY CAT BLUES
SCOTCH COWBOY
SCRUB, SCRUB
SHE WORKS THIRD TUB AT THE
  LAUNDRY
SHE'S DONE AND GONE AWAY
SHOOT ME DEAD FOR THAT ONE
SING A LITTLE SONG ABOUT ANYTHING
SINGIN' MY CARES AWAY
SLOOP, SLOOP, SLOOP
SMART ALECK CROW
SMILE AGAIN HONEY
SMILING
SMITHY'S A LIAR
SOME DANCIN'
SOMEDAY IN WYOMING (WYOMING
  WALTZ)
SOMEONE SWELL
SONG OF THE TRAIL
SPOOKY MOUNTAIN SALLY
SUNSET HILL
SURE SOUNDS GOOD TO ME
THE STILLS IN THE HILLS ARE STILL
  TONIGHT
SWAMP WOMAN BLUES

T'AIN'T WORTH IT
THAT OLD CREAM FREEZER
THAT OLD TEXAS TRAIL IS CALLING ME
THAT WAS ME BY THE SEA
THAT'S ALL BROTHER, THAT'S ALL
THAT'S HOW DONKEYS WERE BORN
THERE'S A LITTLE CEDAR CHEST IN
  THE ATTIC
THERE'S NOTHIN' LIKE WORK
THEY GOT ME BOYS, THEY GOT ME
THEY WON'T PAY ME
THIEVIN' BURRO, THE
TONIGHT'S MY NIGHT TO HOWL
TOP IT
TRAVELIN' MAN
TRICKY SENOR
TROUBADOUR OF THE PLAINS, THE
TROMBONE SONG
TWENTY LONG YEARS
TWISTER
UNCLE HENRY'S VACATION
UNCLE NOAH'S ARK
VITAMIN D
WAGON TRAIN
WASHBOARD AND ROOM
WAY DOWN LOW
WAY DOWN ON THE BOTTOM
WAY OUT WEST IN IDAHO
WE CAN USE THE THING IN HEAVEN
WESTERN LULLABY
WHAT? NO HAWSES IN HEAVEN?
WHEN THE MOON SHINES ON THE
  MISSISSIPPI VALLEY
WHEN YOU GO
WHERE WILL THE WEDDING SUPPER
  BE?
WHO DON'T?
WIND SINGS A COWBOY SONG, THE
WHO'D A THUNK IT
WITH MY LUCK
WOOING OF KITTY McFOOTY, THE
WOULDN'T YOU LIKE TO KNOW?
YAHOO (COVERED WAGON COFFEE)
YODELER, THE
YOU CAN TAKE THE BOY OUT OF THE
  COUNTRY
YOU CAN KEEP ME IN THE SADDLE
YOU CAN'T DO IT
YOU DON'T LOOK LIKE THE PICTURE
YOU PUT ME ON MY FEET
YOU'RE NOT LIKE YOU USED TO BE
YOU'VE GOT TO BE MORE EXCLUSIVE
  WITH ME

BURNETTE AND JOHN CASON

John Cason's demeanor didn't fool any B-Western hero (1941-53). Upon concluding mid-1940s PRC B-villainy against oats star Buster Crabbe, Cason joined *The Durango Kid* series in early Fall 1946 for shooting on THE LONE HAND TEXAN (Columbia, 1947) where he sternly ordered a befuddled Smiley Burnette to begin digging his own grave upon their first screen encounter. John did 11 additional Durangos that included THE KID FROM BROKEN GUN (Columbia, 1952), the final series entry. *(photo courtesy of Boyd Magers)*

SMILEY SNIPPETS

Smiley was first called Frog in the 1935 Republic picture MELODY TRAIL.

He sings his song "Ridin' Down the Canyon" behind the credits of the 1935 Reb Russell film, CHEYENNE TORNADO.

He appeared in one movie with George O'Brien: THE BORDER PATROLMAN (20th Century-Fox, 1936).

Although it is claimed he changed his name to Smiley, the California Death Database and the Social Security Death Database lists his name as Lester Burnette.

The black ring, painted on his white horse, was always around his horse's left eye.

He once received an award from the National Safety Council for having worn out 27 cars without ever being involved in an accident.

Comic book publisher Magazine Enterprises issued The Durango Kid comic books which featured a sidekick called "Muley" Pike. Muley is a Smiley Burnette look-a-like. Many wondered why Smiley was not in these comic books. It is because the company only licensed Charles Starrett and The Durango Kid. At the time, Smiley was licensed by the Fawcett comic book company so he could not appear in the Durango comics.

Smiley was once arrested. While appearing in Orlando, Florida, Smiley was incarcerated for not paying the tax required by those performing in the city. He was not aware of such a law and refused to pay the fine. He spent the night in jail — in an unlocked cell. The next morning, Smiley pleaded his case before a judge claiming the law did not apply to him because he was teaching children. After Smiley demonstrated his act, the judge concurred and the case was dismissed.

He once owned a chain of restaurants called "The Checkered Shirt." Smiley was the first to build a restaurant in the shape of an A-Frame.

Smiley appeared in pictures with "river" in the title — one for Republic and four at Columbia.

He never owned a horse.

He was honored with a star on the Hollywood Walk of Fame at 6125 Hollywood Boulevard on May 22, 1986 (nearly 20 years after his death).

It is estimated Smiley made nearly 10,000 personal appearances. He once said, "I'm a poor man's Bob Hope."

Publisher and Western film historian Boyd Magers rated Burnette number two of all the sidekicks — behind Gabby Hayes.

Smiley appeared in 57 Autry B-Western features.

His original hat and shirt were donated to the National Cowboy Hall of Fame in Oklahoma City, Oklahoma, in 1962.

After his children were grown, he and Dallas lived in, and often traveled in, a mobile home.

Smiley became a member of the Christian Scientist religion due to his wife. Smiley had taken a tumble from a horse and suffered with serious back pain for a couple of years. The pain became so severe that he was open to anything that might help. His wife, already a Christian Scientist, inquired if he would try a Christian Scientist practitioner. He did, and he awoke the next morning without pain. That night the pain returned and the practitioner was called again, and from that time on he had no more back pain.

While Gene Autry was in the service, he told Johnny Bond, "I'm not going to use Frog in future pictures ... Not only him, but Republic as well ... William S. Hart never used a comic. Neither did Tom Mix, Buck Jones or any of the rest of them. I don't know if I need one or not. If I do though, I have a guy in mind, Sterling Holloway. He hasn't been in Westerns, but we can dress him for the part. Besides, I like him. He has the 'Stepin Fetchit' look about him, and he enlisted in service. I'm going to stay with the patriots because, when this thing is over, I think the public is going to remember who served and who didn't."

In August 1958, Smiley's cookbook was taken on the top secret voyage of the USS NAUTILUS by Commander William R. Anderson. This voyage was the first crossing of the North Pole by a ship—a nuclear powered submarine. He received a letter from Anderson: "Dear Smiley, I thought you might enjoy knowing that a copy of your wonderful book you gave us made the first trip in history of a ship to the North Pole, passing under the Pole on August 3, 1958. Perhaps you should have included a couple of Eskimo recipes! Best Regards, "Andy" William R. Anderson."

Smiley enjoyed many foods, but he did not like spinach and watermelon.

He was considered a gourmet cook and when he stayed with acquaintances while on tours, he would often prepare a meal. His pancakes were a specialty.

Smiley Burnette's Buttermilk Pancakes

2 Cups Flour
2 Cups Buttermilk
1 Teaspoon Baking Soda
1 Teaspoon Baking Powder
1/2 Teaspoon Salt
1 Tablespoon Sugar
1 Egg

Mix in blender (if too thick, add more buttermilk); pour into container and refrigerate overnight. In morning pour small spoonfuls onto hot griddle and cook until edges are lacy. Turn once.

Smiley Burnette and Eddie Dew are on guard against outlaws while filming Republic's *John Paul Revere* series in 1943.

PAT BUTTRAM AND THE CANNON
(From *Western Clippings* #27 — published by Boyd Magers)

I thought it important to include the following reports of Buttram's injury, since it was the injury that made it possible for Smiley to end his film career the way it started — with Gene Autry.

Pat Buttram nearly died when a supposed rainmaker's cannon blew up, ripping open Pat's chest and stomach. It was about 6:00 p.m. at Pioneertown during the filming of the TV episode, "The Peacemaker" (originally titled "The Scorched Earth.") The prop man had picked up a bronze antique cannon—about three feet long on wooden wheels. There was no licensed powder man available, so the prop man rigged a small pan of flash powder at the bottom (rather than taping it to the top of the cannon), then covered the wire with dirt so it wouldn't show as it was led behind a rock where he was to set off the charge. When Pat pulled the string trigger, the prop man tripped his wire and the powder inside the cannon literally exploded like a bomb, throwing shrapnel all over the area. Pat was less than three feet away. One large piece hit Pat in the chest, another in the jaw and a large chunk cut through his left boot, severing an artery. Shrapnel whizzed past Gene's head, but Champion was nicked above one eye. One wrangler had his knee broken, and a second man was hit. Pat's entire chest was cut open, and he was losing blood quickly in his boot. Loading Pat in a pickup truck, they rushed down the hill to Gene's airplane.

Gene's pilot, Herb Green, flew to Twenty-nine Palms for a doctor. Green would be flying at night so Gene and the rest phoned ahead as there were no lights on the tiny airport's runway. The telephone operator called all over town and people jumped in their cars and drove to the airfield, turning on their lights allowing Green to land the plane. As soon as Dr. Bill Ince (son of movie pioneer Thomas Ince, who'd produced William S. Hart Westerns) was flown back from Twenty-nine Palms, he began to work on Pat. Immediately putting a clamp on the severed artery and picking shrapnel and dirt from Pat's open chest wound, all while Pat was conscious. Before an ambulance arrived, Green made more hurried flights—one to bring plasma and another to fly in a second doctor from Los Angeles to assist Ince. Pat was laid up for nine months. Sheila Ryan, who he'd been dating, moved to Twenty-nine Palms to be near him. When he was on his feet again, they were married.

(Miss Ryan had been previously married to Allan "Rocky" Lane, Republic B-Western star from 1944 to 1953.)

Gene Autry describes the accident:

We were making a picture up at Pioneertown—the TV show, actually—and Pat was supposed to be a rainmaker. He had a cannon, and he was supposed to shoot it up in the clouds to make it rain. So someone that day overloaded that cannon. It had a nozzle inside of it—it was brass. It had been turned inside to make it round looking. And, the special effects guy put too much powder in that thing. I was sitting closest on a horse, as close as you and I are here, and they set the fuse off on that cannon, and it backfired. I guess when he went in there, he must have closed up that nozzle of the barrel, and it backfired, and it blew old Pat halfway to hell—just tore his guts out. And, part of the shrapnel from that thing came and hit my old horse in the nose and in the shoulder, and a part of it just nearly passed my head, and if it had hit me, why it'd probably have killed me, or cut my head off. So, it was just that close. That's an accident, of course. None of those things are ever intended to happen, but they do. And it just so happened that at that time we were finishing up on the series that we had going. I forget how many it was, 26 I guess it was—and then we brought in Chill Wills. He did some of them, and then we brought in Fuzzy Knight, and he did some of them. And then we kind of rewrote a lot of them after that, but the reason we had to have a comedy relief was because those scripts were already finished, and we used Chill in four of them, and we used Fuzzy Knight in about four, and that give us eight, and I think that finished the series. We were off then. We had a hiatus of two or three months and then, by that time, Pat could come back in again.

Pat Buttram about to drink water from a pail.

GENE AUTRY ON STRIKE

by Richard B. Smith III

Since Smiley Burnette was so closely associated with Gene Autry, and since whatever happened with Autry also affected Smiley, Gene's strikes against Republic should be of interest to Smiley's fans. The following two articles initially appeared in **Western Clippings** *#27 and #35.*

THE FIRST STRIKE

What follows is a detailed account with respect to singing movie cowboy Gene Autry's initial legal dispute at Republic which lasted 60 days during mid-1936 before he made OH, SUSANNA! The other long, drawn out, hot feuds Autry had against Republic would attract attention in *Variety* and *Hollywood Reporter* in 1937-'38, 1945-'47 and 1952-'55. Part of Gene's *modus operandi* in his first two big battles was to hastily exit Studio City for an extended personal appearance tour and line up other possible paying projects that eventually forced Republic to initiate extensive court action against him. Once Republic and Autry were reunited, acceptable terms for a new contract would be just about always in the maverick cowboy's favor.

Autry signatured his initial feature contract with Mascot on May

17, 1935. Then President Nat Levine merged his small movie company June 11, into the new Republic Pictures Corporation which had officially organized March 28, 1935. Autry's three-year pact was immediately transferred to Republic whereby he was paid $100 each week for eight annual B-westerns with six-month options involving $50 raises. Gene's association at the freshman studio went smoothly during the premier 1935-36 season through his 8th oatuner, GUNS AND GUITARS, May 9, 1936. Immediately, Autry began complaining that the small salary he earned from Republic was not in line with his studio value. The singing cowboy also reacted negatively at making a 9th Western, OH, SUSANNA!, before his picture season officially ended June 30, 1936.

Meanwhile, Republic ordered Gene to report to the film set May 20. Autry, instead, left Sunday evening May 17 for a three-month personal appearance tour to include Texas, Oklahoma and other southern states. He prepared these schedules on the premise Republic was unwilling to discuss contractual revisions. Autry's speedy departure caught the studio off guard and, up to that point, without any Western stars to work the new 1936-37 season. Action lead John Wayne was already headed for Universal after winding up his one-season filming stint with WINDS OF THE WASTELAND on May 11.

Thinking ahead, Gene also thought of participation in radio as well as personals that could gross him approximately $1,000 per week in both entertainment mediums. The singer was set to reach New York City and negotiate a stage tour for Fall 1936. Additionally, allegedly, he became receptive to film offers from other movie outfits of around $3,500 per picture.

Meantime, Republic stopped Gene Autry's tour at Pittsburg, Kansas on May 26 with a federal court restraining order. May 29's temporary injunction followed. The cowboy reportedly had issued warnings earlier to skedaddle down Mexico way and get in Westerns there. But these court rulings kept Gene stateside as well as not being able to engage in other show business ventures apart from his Republic contract. The studio wanted $9,444.37 from Autry, the amount it claimed, already spent for preparation of OH, SUSANNA! A show-cause hearing to make the original federal order permanent was postponed to June 9, as Autry had not been found for presentation of his summons.

Meanwhile, the temporary restraint remained in effect. Responding in federal court June 5 to Republic producer Nat Levine that his services were not special or unique, Autry, acting through attorneys Goldenhorn and Komins denied a boast concerning United States departure and, since the movie period wasn't set until July 1, he informed Republic of this impending tour which it supposedly approved. Gene also asserted a separate oral contract (with production manager Sol Siegel) maintained the cowboy was not obligated for more than the allotted number of movies.

On June 16, Federal Judge William James ordered the temporary injunction remain against Gene, provided Republic post a $20,000 bond within five days. Now, Autry wanted $900 back wages from the studio coffers, plus $1,000 per week for the period of personal appearances interrupted unwarrantedly. An ironclad restraining order was lodged against Republic's miscreant June 19. However, by late June, Judge James amended his previous ruling in the studio's injunction giving Gene an opportunity to make phonograph recordings and appear on radio. James set July 2 for deciding the possible permanent injunction as Gene was to be Chicago-bound to discuss a radio hookup with Sears Roebuck.

Republic entered general denial July 1 to every Autry counterclaim. Despite excessive finger pointing and wagging of tongues from opposing sides over a two-month period, both came together July 7, and settled their differences, resulting in court-action dismissal. Autry and Republic smoked the peace pipe July 8. The cowboy signed a fresh seven-year contract to mainline eight pictures every 365 days that allowed Republic the right for two more movies from Autry as added compensation, and a weekly salary rise with yearly increases.

(Author Holly George-Warren's 2007 biography, Public Cowboy No. 1—The Life and Times of Gene Autry, *reveals updated salary disclosures of July 8, 1936, that Autry, at the time, converted from his weekly term-contract player status to a $2,000 per-picture arrangement starting with OH, SUSANNA! (1936). When Gene began filming BOOTS AND SADDLES (1937), his pay was now $5,000 for each new musical B-Western he made for Republic.)*

Gene couldn't make outside features under this new arrangement, but had the right to all proceeds from personal appearances, radio, records and music publishing. Four days later (July 12, 1936), Republic cameras rolled as OH, SUSANNA! got the gun from director Joseph Kane.

An unfortunate accident occurred July 14 in the Kernville vicinity when several cast members were shaken up aboard their bus after overturning on a soft shoulder. Associate producer Bob Beche sustained several injuries—a broken arm, cuts and bruises that resulted in admittance to a Bakersfield hospital. Five other passengers required medical assistance.

Additional away-from-studio locations utilized were Lone Pine, Iverson's Ranch and Lang railroad depot in the Saugus area. Shooting on Republic's backlot for this highly-charged, fast-paced production has Gene within the Western town set, where during a long take, he walks hurriedly by contemporary signs advertising Butterfinger, Lipton Tea, and Champion spark plugs.

OH, SUSANNA! wrapped up July 18, 1936, with an approximate negative cost of $25,000. OH, SUSANNA! began a new format for Autry oatuners, employing various cowboy music groups, usually regional, with at least some radio fame. The Light Crust Doughboys, out of Fort Worth, were first according to Gene in his autobiography, *Back In the Saddle Again* (1978). Autry wrote, "Music in my previous films had been supplied by Smiley, myself, and a few, uncredited backup musicians."

(The bass fiddle player recognized in several music interludes with the Doughboys was talented Bert Dodson, who became part of the famous Cass County Boys trio some years later. The Doughboys, who'd appear the last time with Autry in his 11th starrer, THE BIG SHOW (1936), organized in 1930. One of their earliest members was Bob Wills before he headed the Texas Playboys.)

THE SECOND STRIKE

The following cites the extensive details of Gene's lengthy strike against Republic and the personal aggravation he endured, both mental and physical, that encompassed his productions of THE OLD BARN DANCE (1938) and GOLD MINE IN THE SKY (1938).

Despite an earlier walk off the Republic lot from mid-May to mid-July 1936, when he was successful in obtaining higher earnings, Gene Autry's contractual relations with the studio had been basically smooth since 1935 for his first 19 starring oatuners through September 1937.

Two months afterwards (November 27, 1937), Autry left for Lone Pine with others to commence acting under Joe Kane's direction in his 20th vehicle, THE OLD BARN DANCE. The next day the film unit shifted over to Kernville for two days of location shooting, then returned to the Republic backlot with accidental chaos becoming routine in many scenes.

On November 30, a much too realistically staged mob fight involving principals and 200 extras went awry. Gene Autry suffered a badly wrenched shoulder, sidekick Smiley Burnette a sprained left wrist, and Colorado Hillbillies' fiddler Robert Hoag fractured his right leg.

The picture resumed its rough-and-tumble incidents on December 2, as a mob scene developed into a battle royale. Stuntman/bit actor Fred Kennedy's foot was stomped on by a horse, player Bill Cowdrey sustained a mashed foot as two horses jammed together, and old-timer Fred Burns received a badly wounded arm after a broken buckboard threw him to the ground. Forty of the bunched horses in some scenes were caught up in the riotous frenzy, stampeding into a residential district back of the lot. When North Hollywood police failed to catch the four-legged steeds, all of Republic's cowhands pitched in to corral them.

With action now toned down, sound-stage scenes concluded lensing for THE OLD BARN DANCE (December 9, 1937) at a negative cost at just over $50,000. A turn of events in late 1937 soured Gene against Republic. Not only was the movie cowboy desirous of more folding money, due to big box-office profits his low-budget Westerns were reaping, but Gene wanted to amend his contract to guarantee Republic wouldn't attempt to collect half the money he made from endorsements, radio, or personal appearances. Also, after hearing one movie distributor complain that a whole Republic film season package was required for purchase in order to obtain eight Gene Autry features, Autry immediately demanded Republic President Herbert J. Yates quit such a policy and listen to his other complaints. Yates refused.

Gene did not show up for the first day's shooting (December 27, 1937) on WASHINGTON COWBOY, which caused his immediate suspension from Republic. He later claimed an appearance two days' hence for camera chores, but said no screenplay was prepared, which resulted in a contract breach. Reportedly, Gene gave the studio until January 5 to start a new film.

Now officially on strike, he headed out on a personal tour of the southwest and midwest, always one step ahead of the process server with a subpoena. *Daily Variety* and *Variety* (January 18, 1938) printed Autry's gripes as Republic and the cowboy had attorneys arguing their respective behalves. Paramount and 20th Century-Fox were ready to best Republic's top offer to Gene for new musical Westerns if he were free to make such a deal.

As January progressed, Autry was willing to exchange peace overtures with the studio if it met his monetary demand to offset the financial loss he incurred in an earlier two-picture Paramount deal before his walkout. Autry squeezed in a New York City trip to negotiate a 32-week circus deal at $4,000 every seven days.

By January 26, Gene's feud with Republic widened even further as the cowboy wired a statement from Nashville refuting studio claims his pictures weren't moneymakers and "Republic, if it wants to make adjustments with exhibitors, can get more money for my releases and still sell its other product at reasonable prices."

A Nashville court judge stymied Gene further on January 27, issuing an injunction requested by Republic's attorneys to restrain him from appearing in films, vaudeville, radio, or stage shows until his present studio contract was concluded. Gene circumvented this for awhile by having the other members of his troupe and his horse on stage while he paid his admission like any other patron and held receptions for the customers in the foyer. The system was not overly successful, as theatre managers felt uneasy in the realization they were outwitting a federal court. *Daily Variety* (January 31, 1938) stated Yates was willing to allow Autry to buy his remaining Republic pact if he apologized for the Nashville statement. But should Autry fail to comply, Yates said he would follow through on legal proceedings, and reminded that the studio had already invested $500,000 in him.

Burned up with the injunction, Autry lost another round February 2 in a Nashville federal court when it refused to dissolve the legal restraint. Autry waited in limbo, but eventually by mid-March, was negotiating with Republic's Yates, probably Sol Siegel and distribution chief James Grainger.

At this point, Gene made some money outside the bounds of

the Republic dispute upon the sale of his three and one-half acre Olive Street ranch in Burbank to Cinecolor Incorporated for construction of a new film laboratory. Unless Republic met his salary demands by April 9, Gene was prepared to trek to South America on a 20-week tour not covered by the U.S. injunction. Such a trip never materialized.

On April 21, the cowboy was back in Nashville to await statements from Yates and Republic executive Moe Siegel in a new effort to dissolve the injunction. Although its results were not mentioned in the trades, this hitch must have been settled satisfactorily, as by May 2 the studio commenced its four-day annual Hollywood sales convention at the Roosevelt Hotel, promoting its 1938-39 product, including eight Autry Westerns. Republic film distributors howled about the six-month famine in Autry movies and wanted assurance from Yates himself that the cowboy was on the studio's payroll for the next year.

The night of May 2, Gene had a serious discussion with Yates and Secretary-treasurer George C. Schaefer. Two days later, Republic convention delegates cheered the cowboy's official return to Republic ranks where he publicly buried the hatchet in a rousing ceremony by walking on stage arm-in-arm with Yates. Gene's new and better terms with Republic resulted in big salary raises. Starting with the 1938-39 season, he was to be paid $6,000 each for the first two pictures and $10,000 per film on the remainder.

Anxious to realize big bucks once again on Gene's movies, Republic wasted no time placing him back in the saddle with his initial post-strike feature, GOLD MINE IN THE SKY. He formally returned to work for recording of this oater's tunes, then left 72 hours later for Keen Camp with 80 other players.

Lensing under direction of Joe Kane got rolling May 21, 1938. During one fight scene, Gene cut his legs from a horse fall so badly that infection resulted in bed confinement at his home under a physician's care. It was five days before he could act once more.

Other location exteriors found the troupe at Garner Ranch, Lake Hemet, San Jacinto Mountains, the Republic backlot and probably the Lang railroad depot northeast of Saugus. With its hectic camera pace, GOLD MINE IN THE SKY ended June 9, 1938, with a negative cost of just below $60,000.

The strike proved very profitable to Gene. Smiley got his scheduled increases, but nothing compared to Gene. Gene had been under a three-year contract from July 1, 1935, through June 30, 1938, which included six-month options. This was a Mascot contract which was transferred to Republic at the time of the formation of that studio (from the merger of Mascot, Monogram, Consolidated Film Laboratories, et al, in 1935). Gene's initial salary was $100 weekly.

Autry was then signed to annual contracts:
- 1938-39: $6,000 for each of the first two films, followed by $10,000 for each of the remainder.
- 1940-41: $11,000 per picture
- 1941-42: $12,000 per picture
- 1942-43: $13,000 per picture. (Only three of the eight films for this current season were made before Autry left for WW2 service. After the war, he returned to Republic and completed five more films at $15,000 per picture according to Boyd Magers' 2007 book, *Gene Autry Westerns*. He then formed his own production company, releasing his B-Westerns via Columbia Pictures.)

POPULARITY RANKINGS OF SMILEY

Thanks to Les Adams

Year	*Motion Picture Herald* Poll Ranking	*Box-office* Poll Ranking
1939		9th
1940	9th	7th
1941	5th	6th
1942	4th	5th
1943	3rd	no poll conducted
1944	3rd	5th
1945	5th	
1946	5th	6th
1947	7th	6th
1948	9th	6th
1949	9th	8th
1950	9th	8th
1951	7th	7th
1952	7th	8th

BURNETTE AT REPUBLIC AND COLUMBIA
— An Analysis —

by Richard B. Smith III

REPUBLIC — 1935-1944

Smiley Burnette, the Illinois native who became so professionally adept at mastering what seemed like an endless array of musical instruments, began his B-Western movie career as Texas-born Gene Autry's sidekick in 1934 with Mascot Pictures, a small Hollywood film corporation. Autry was already achieving national popularity as a radio singer when he and Burnette made brief croon debuts for veteran B-oats stars Ken Maynard's IN OLD SANTA FE (1934) at Mascot, that studio's only B-Western.

Following MYSTERY MOUNTAIN (Mascot, 1934), the 12-chapter serial also with Maynard, and Autry's elevation as star in THE PHANTOM EMPIRE (Mascot, 1935), also a chapterplay, Smiley was absorbed with Gene into the new Republic Pictures Corporation that was organized during late March 1935. Guiding its development was Consolidated Film Laboratories President Herbert J. Yates. Other small movie outfits included in the final formation /merger with Mascot were

Liberty, Chesterfield, and Monogram.

Burnette's 1st co-starring Republic B-Western with Gene Autry was TUMBLING TUMBLEWEEDS (1935). This was a landmark Hollywood movie that began the singing cowboy film trend. Such an idea for music in sagebrushers sung by the hero was Yates' brainstorm. And it would prove so popular in many B-Westerns well into the 1950s with profitable box-office receipts.

Smiley's original Mascot term-player contract was not transferred to Republic until July 1, 1936. Whether Burnette ever reflected on his good fortune at Republic in partnering in Gene Autry B-oatuners, and how well such Westerns were produced with their endless quality despite restricted budgets, one will never know.

Smiley Burnette busily made 50 B-Westerns at Republic with Gene Autry in addition to six starring with Roy Rogers, two with Eddie Dew, three as saddlemate to Bob Livingston, and four with Sunset Carson. In 64 of the 65 B-Westerns, he portrayed Frog Millhouse, saddlemate and singer of humorous melodies.

All his Republic movies were lensed between July 6, 1935 and July 3, 1944, ranging in rounded-off negative costs of $20,000 to $135,000. Shooting days were anywhere from 6 to 20 plus on each lensing. Additionally, others between the shoot-em-ups that Smiley appeared in were two Republic serials and nine studio features of different genres from late 1935 into mid-Summer 1938.

It is an established fact that Smiley Burnette played well with Autry, because both entertainers loved Western music. Additionally, Smiley was in a majority of the movie scenes with Gene and certainly had the latitude for his comic performances liberally granted by Republic's screenwriters.

But once Autry exited Republic for military service in July 1942, the movie studio returned Smiley to Roy Rogers' musical B-Westerns, a wise move as Rogers was a natural actor and excellent cowboy-tunes singer to whom Burnette could relate with emoting and warbling.

Then a mystery suddenly emerged. Burnette, for no explainable reason, was suddenly yanked from the Rogers $130,000-costing features, and placed in a new all-action *John Paul Revere* series starring Eddie Dew that would limit Smiley to one song for each of his final Republic Western movies.

Continuing the same Burnette role as Frog Millhouse with Dew and then Bob Livingston through end of 1943 filming, he did the parts okay, but there wasn't the mutual chemistry as there had been with Autry and Rogers.

Coming onto the Republic lot then early in 1944 was a 23-year-old Texas/Oklahoma rodeo cowboy, and 6'4" to boot, named Michael Harrison (real name Winifred Maurice Harrison) whom Yates changed to Sonny "Sunset" Carson. With only two non-Western movies, STAGE DOOR CANTEEN (United Artists, 1943) and JANIE (Warner Bros., 1944), as experience, Carson had been tapped to succeed Bob Livingston in starring B-Western action roles. He was co-starred with Smiley Burnette whose name was first in opening credits, something no other movie cowboy sidekick was to accomplish.

Once you view CALL OF THE ROCKIES (Republic, 1944), their initial movie in the *Superior Westerns* series, there was this sense of tremendous camaraderie developing between Burnette and Carson. They just clicked well as a twosome! Smiley hadn't looked so happy and content since the earlier screen times he had with Gene Autry and Roy Rogers.

But then Burnette would do only three more outdoor B-adventures with Carson at Republic. It was rumored at end of June 1944, just prior to the time Smiley was to renew his Republic contract, that he was not willing to continue acting at the studio without Autry.

The other more important factor for his firm decision to exit Republic at the time possibly was salary related. It has been unsubstantiated that instead of the $1000 per week he was allegedly earning on a 40-week related basis as stated by late author Jack Mathis in *Republic Confidential (Volume 2 — The Players)*, published in 1992, Smiley was just earning $1,000 per B-Western per week whenever he was actually filming.

If the latter salary set-up was correct since about 1939, then Burnette had plenty of reason in wanting to transfer his talents to some other movie studio in the mid-1940s. The exact reason for Smiley departing Republic may never be known.

However, for this talented film comic to suddenly up and quit Republic without any prospect of another studio contract was a very risky proposition for him at best. Of course, Smiley could rely upon personal appearance tours as a venue for continued revenue.

COLUMBIA — 1945-1953

Roughly six months was to elapse before Smiley finally signed with the major Columbia Pictures in early January 1945. According to Smiley's son Stephen, Smiley signed a 10-year pact at the studio, and he obtained an understanding from Columbia President Harry Cohn that once in *The Durango Kid* series with star Charles Starrett that he — Burnette — would assist with writing the script, comedy relief, and songs.

Despite the supposed Cohn/Burnette agreement, approximately another four months was to go by before Smiley officially began co-starring with Starrett that involved a significant salary increase, evidently more money than during his Republic days.

While he began camera duties in mid-May 1945 on *The Durango Kid* sagebrushers with ROARING RANGERS (Columbia, 1946), Burnette was to discover the much bigger Columbia set-up with respect to quality low-budget motion pictures far different then when riding the camera range at Republic Pictures.

This was the reason! Columbia head Harry Cohn commanded a vast money-making operation. Cohn, only interested in five or six top film-moneymaker releases for Columbia per year, was green-lighting multi-million dollar productions, such as THE JOLSON STORY (Columbia, 1947) in Technicolor, costing $2.5 million, being lensed with shooting times of 3 to 5 months. Several of these lavish tinters, also cameraed with Technicolor, starred alluring Rita Hayworth, Cohn's pet actress.

While such features were Cohn's annual prides and joys, he severely ridiculed the studio's B-unit product terming the pictures "junk," but used such box-office profits from them to finance the big Columbia A-films. Cohn's negative appraisals about the Bs took in serials, B-action and musical Westerns, plus regular B-movie series at that time such as *Blondie, The Crime Doctor, The Whistler, Boston Blackie, The Lone Wolf, Rusty,* and later during 1948 with the start of production on *Jungle Jim*. Then there were also individual B-dramas, and two-reel comedy shorts such as "The Three Stooges."

Charles Starrett's *Durango Kid* series were the cheapest produced Columbia pictures of the mid-1940s since they had the least shooting days of any Columbia B-films. Negative cost on each one, according to late Columbia director Earl Bellamy, was estimated in the $50,000 - $55,000 category.

Smiley Burnette was to portray himself, not Frog Millhouse from his Republic years because the studio possessed rights to that character name.

Starrett, himself, was a solid Columbia veteran star going back to 1935, as successor to horse-opera ace Tim McCoy, having done 67 B-Westerns before commencing *The Durango Kid* series on a consistent lensing basis in early June 1944. Charles Starrett was a handsome gentleman and fine actor, and fast talker with dialogue, but also possessed a broad, beaming smile. An adept horseman, Starrett could fan the hammer on his pistol for quick gunfire better than any other movie cowboy in the B-Western era.

The debut Durango sagebrusher was appropriately titled THE RETURN OF THE DURANGO KID (Columbia, 1945). Its predecessor was simply named THE DURANGO KID (Columbia, 1940) and was filmed 46 months earlier during August 1940.

In the initial 1944-45 production season of filming, Starrett's sidekicks were player Tex Harding and longtime saddle comic Dub Taylor. Harding was an ex-U. S. Marine Corps veteran, a plenty capable actor, and a fine rider, possessing the same thespian talents of ex-Columbia B-Western star Russell Hayden from the early 1940s. Harding was reportedly "a bit unmanageable and somewhat of a drinker," according to publisher Boyd Magers (*Western Clippings* #57, January/February 2004).

Recent information (late 2003) indicates that Harding's singing voice may have been dubbed and the real voice doing Tex's songs belonged to James T. "Bud" Nelson (born January 28, 1914, Brooklyn, New York, passed away March 13, 1994, Las Vegas, Nevada). Nelson did appear on screen in bit and background roles in several of *The Durango Kid* films.

Dub Taylor had the unlikely character moniker of Cannonball. He was a seasoned Columbia player since 1939 in the movie outfit's low-budget horse operas where he began to duo with Bill Elliott, then partnered next to Russell Hayden and Charles Starrett.

Taylor also possessed the maddening habit of constantly falling down after tripping over himself in many of the movies for Columbia. Taylor did 7 of the first 8 Durangos in 1944-45.

Also, the first Durangos saw three of them not lensed in order of their National Release Dates. Thusly, TEXAS PANHANDLE (Columbia, 1945) became the last camera appearance of Tex Harding and Dub Taylor, the latter not connecting up to a new B-Western series for 25 1/2 months until June 1947 when he was placed again as sidekick Cannonball in the continuing Jimmy Wakely cowboy films at Monogram Pictures.

Canceling Harding's part was a big mistake by Columbia as Charles Starrett needed the partnering strength of a regular male player with him instead of just relying on dialogue exchange with a Western comic.

It is apparent that Taylor and Harding both were dropped by Columbia with the studio having decided much earlier in 1945 what these two players' fates would be once Smiley Burnette was contracted. It appears that the combined salaries of Harding/Taylor were turned over to Burnette who may have pulled in even more money.

With TEXAS PANHANDLE wrapping film duty May 9, 1945, Smiley immediately entered his first Durango with Starrett, ROARING RANGERS (Columbia, 1946), that commenced shooting eight days later.

Big negatives confronting Burnette once he faced lenses at Columbia were the following:

1. The first was Smiley's fault. He told Starrett that he was put into the Durangos while filming GUNNING FOR VENGEANCE (Columbia, 1946) because the pictures weren't doing too well at the box office and that they needed "a shot in the arm." Such remarks did not set well with Starrett as their relationship would remain chilly and strained on future features until they really got to know one another.

2. Stock footage use was prolific from earlier years' movies that made the current Durangos shown even more cheaper with such insertions.

3. No really big-name music groups such as Bob Wills and His Texas Playboys were used to back up Smiley on his songs. The only group exception to this statement was the Cass County Boys who had proven acting/singing experience in Gene Autry's final five Republic Pictures releases of the 1946-47 period. The Cass County Boys probably had

one- and two-picture deals with Columbia for Durangos as did 14 other different music groups that appeared with Starrett/Burnette.

4. Such proliferation of singers gave them about 5-10 minutes of movie fame, but probably did nothing to boost their overall careers into the big time thus confusing movie audiences as to who was actually a regular music group for Starrett/Burnette. Smiley did sing at times with these groups and wrote/sang himself an average of two to three new songs per Durango. Columbia knew it could hire much lesser-known musicians at reduced pay to remain within the standard budget for each succeeding Starrett. By not having Bob Wills and His Texas Playboys stay in the series, it meant that Columbia wouldn't have to delve deeper into its studio coffers.

5. Studio sets were very meager and cheap in appearance such as viewed for offices, saloons and shacks, but were somewhat better for living room scenes.

6. Filming times on each of these B-Westerns were usually no longer than 7 to 9 days. Durangos such as LAST DAYS OF BOOT HILL (Columbia, 1947) and CYCLONE FURY (Columbia, 1951) had lesser lensing times by inserting expanded minutes of earlier Durango footage.

7. A typical Durango would commence with grainy recycled stock footage, then some scenes leading to a plot line, musical entertainment; next was action and shooting sequences by Durango followed by comedy or music from Smiley, then additional plotting by the bad guys, etc. Such repetitious cycles would occur and occur over again several times. There was never any respectable continuity to the Durangos.

8. A huge drawback added to these movies were Columbia's screenwriters' meticulous but ridiculous insistence that Charles Starrett's first name character of Steve was to have a different last name for each succeeding B-Western as if

that were ever to make any real impression on the movie audiences of the mid-1940s until the early 1950s.

9. Another major detriment for these screen adventures was sighting Charles Starrett quickly riding his dark horse Lightning out of camera range at different times in a Durango feature to suddenly reappear in his all-black Durango Kid outfit with mask and astride white mount Raider. Starrett would emerge from behind a boulder on location at either Corriganville, Iverson Ranch, or Providencia Ranch, or from a town barn at Columbia Ranch. This was certainly overworking movie fantasy for the Saturday-matinee kids, but they probably enjoyed such fakery for its pure-fun elements anyway.

Once on board at Columbia with a steady production pace on the Durangos and his white horse renamed Ringeye, Smiley sang his composed tunes and acted out minimal professions assigned. (For more detail on Burnette's parts and songs, note Smiley's filmography at conclusion of this analysis.)

Smiley Burnette's Columbia film schedule with onset of the Durangos found him doing the first eight oaters through November 13, 1945, ending on TERROR TRAIL (Columbia, 1946), then laying off for seven months. On June 11, 1946, production resumed for another eight films with Burnette and Starrett finishing them December 17, 1946, during lensing of RIDERS OF THE LONE STAR (Columbia, 1947). It was with this title that Columbia contemplated dropping *The Durango Kid* series, but then reversed course and let these B-Westerns continue.

Beginning May 20, 1947, Starrett/Burnette reunited for a third season of eight additional Durangos with BUCKAROO FROM POWDER RIVER (Columbia, 1947), riding on the lens range until TRAIL TO LAREDO (Columbia, 1948) shooting concluded December 16, 1947.

With Smiley's 25th Durango entry of EL DORADO PASS

(Columbia, 1948) as it commenced lens duties May 8, 1948, the frenetic shooting of Starrett/Burnette B-Westerns with only a week or so break between each production found future Columbia camera hiatuses stretched to as many as three months, no doubt a welcome relief by both actors.

In the meantime, Burnette former co-star Gene Autry had been filming B-Westerns for his Gene Autry Productions with Columbia Pictures release since mid-May 1947. And Autry in early 1950 formed his own Flying A Pictures to film 30-minute horse operas for television.

Gene's comic sidekick, in place of Burnette, was funny-voiced Pat Buttram doing both the Autry movies and the star's half-hour TV shows. Everything was going smooth for Buttram until the latter half of 1950 when he was severely wounded by a misfired cannon that exploded. He sustained metal fragments in the chest and stomach from flying debris while filming a TV episode with Autry and faced long-term recuperation.

Smiley Burnette, at this juncture, had just completed BONANZA TOWN (Columbia, 1951) with Starrett on November 18, 1950. Autry was scheduled to do another Columbia film WHIRLWIND (1951), and hired past saddle pal Burnette to substitute for Buttram in the picture. On December 4, 1950, Smiley and Gene came together again as WHIRLWIND began filming. Eight days later, Smiley was available to rejoin Starrett. That occurred after the Christmas holidays for production resumption of *The Durango Kid* series in early January 1951 with CYCLONE FURY (Columbia, 1951).

Durango sagebrushers, with a total of 64 released since mid-April 1945, came to an official filming end on April 4, 1952, on wind-up of THE KID FROM BROKEN GUN (Columbia, 1952). Following Starrett's 64 appearances as *The Durango Kid*, Burnette trailed as his seven-year partner with 56 movies.

Charles Starrett, perpetually known as the outlaw chaser dressed in an all black outfit including mask, declined to film more entries for the Durango series, or even 30-minute Durango TV episodes, and so, therefore, didn't renew his Columbia Pictures contract because of a physical weariness with the role. He then departed Columbia having done a total of 131 starring B-Westerns for the studio since 1935. Starrett would act in no other features being content to abandon the movie industry for good.

Meantime, Columbia scheduled a new B-Western horse opera series for Burnette to co-star with actor/stuntman Jock Mahoney, a late 1940s Starrett stunter for the Durango Westerns. Mahoney, now "The Range Rider" TV star, had supplemented his acting income by appearing as himself in the final seven Charles Starretts of 1951-52. But any Burnette/Mahoney pairing in features was eventually rescinded by Columbia.

Almost three months following end of Durango production, Smiley Burnette joined Gene Autry to sidekick in what would be the star's concluding six B-Westerns for Columbia release. Smiley reported to the Autry set in late June 1952 for filming on WINNING OF THE WEST (Columbia, 1953).

It was like old times again for Burnette and Autry who made certain his partner did a big number of acting segments for the above feature as well as in the remaining five although Gene's LAST OF THE PONY RIDERS (Columbia, 1953), his last B-Western entry, saw Smiley basically lazying out of motion pictures in an easy fashion.

Whatever one personally thought of Smiley Burnette, his comic talents sustained him over a period of 19 years with popular B-Western cowboy stars. He was not the best rider or actor on screen, but Smiley must be applauded for originality in playing any kind of musical instrument. The highest praise anybody can grant Smiley was his tremendous ability to write tunes on a moment's notice. And he composed so many, I believe it could be difficult to work up an official tally. What a life this man lived in making so many children and adults reach their highest peaks of happiness and laughter.

SMILEY'S FILM ROLES

IN OLD SANTA FE (Mascot, 1934). He joins radio crooner Gene Autry in first supporting role as accordionist/singer. Warbles his and Autry's "Mama Don't Like Music" plus Smiley helps croon "Down In Old Santa Fe," Mascot's only B-Western starring Ken Maynard. Burnette was hired at $35 per week while Autry became salaried with $100 each seven days.

(The copyright title of Smiley's song is "Mama Don't Like No Music." This is how it is published in Smiley's 1937 song book. However, Smiley's version is a take-off on "Cow Cow" Davenport's "Mama Don't Allow No Easy Riders Here." Since Smiley is so closely associated with the song, many have credited him as the originator.)

MYSTERY MOUNTAIN (Mascot, 1934). A 12-chapter Western serial, Smiley's part is that of a teamster, but he and Gene Autry have no songs in this Ken Maynard vehicle.

THE PHANTOM EMPIRE (Mascot, 1935). While Gene Autry is elevated to star here for this 12-chapter science-fiction whodunit about the underworld kingdom of Murania, Smiley takes on the role of Oscar. He hams and sings with William Moore (Peter Potter in later years) as Pete. Both Oscar and Pete characters are mentally deficient as cowboy musicians.

Burnette sings and/or writes "Uncle Noah's Ark," "I'm Oscar, I'm Pete," "No Need to Worry," "Uncle Henry," "I'm Getting a Moon's Eye View of the World," and "Just Come On Back."

TUMBLING TUMBLEWEEDS (Republic,1935). First co-starring musical B-Western at Republic Pictures for Smiley as perpetual partner to Gene Autry in this landmark film. Burnette is in the role of Smiley, strictly feeling his way here as a low-key actor and musician with assertive George Hayes' traveling medicine show. He helps Autry solve the killing of his father Joe Girard murdered for illegal possession of water rights by bad guy Edward Hearn. Smiley also slams a guitar on top of bad guy Charles King's head. Burnette sings and/or accompanies on "Tumbling Tumbleweeds." "Cowboy Medicine Show," boisterously twice with "Corn-Fed and Rusty," "Oh, Susanna," and "That Silver Haired Daddy of Mine."

MELODY TRAIL (Republic, 1935). More animated here, this was Smiley's 1st role in the continuing character of Frog Millhouse that he would continue with Republic filming in B-Westerns through late June 1944. He is suspected of calf rustling by cowgirls who chase him from a meadow, and does a rodeo clown bit at the opening of this oatuner in addition to twitting loudmouth Al Bridge. This was also the debut of Burnette's shrill shout to star Gene Autry of "Hey, Gene! Hey, Gene!" whenever he needed quick assistance of some sort. Also assists Autry with an extensive cooking scene. Sings "Way Down On the Bottom," "Western Lullaby," "My Neighbor Hates Music," and "Where Will the Wedding Supper Be?"

(The Saint Bernard dog Buck was billed above the title with Gene Autry on the original title card and posters. Buck was also in THE CALL OF THE WILD (United Artists, 1935), THE COUNTRY BEYOND (20th Century-Fox, 1936), ROBINSON CRUSOE OF CLIPPER ISLAND (1936 Republic serial), THE TRIGGER TRIO (Republic, 1937, a Three Mesquiteers Republic picture), and THE GENTLEMAN FROM ARIZONA

(Monogram, 1939). Director William Witney said Buck's double Cappy was the best-trained dog he had ever seen.)

SAGEBRUSH TROUBADOUR (Republic, 1935). Burnette is a State Ranger with Autry investigating the murder of leading lady Barbara Pepper's granddad who died of guitar-string strangulation because of a hidden gold mine. Smiley keeps falling off an old swayback horse which brings laughter to any viewer plus plays numerous musical instruments and hits player Frank Glendon with his guitar. He warbles and/or accompanies on "Way Out West In Texas," "On the Prairie," "My Prayer For Tonight," "End of the Trail," "Looking For the Lost Chord," and "I'd Love a Home In the Mountains."

OTHER SMILEY FILM OF 1935

WATERFRONT LADY (Mascot, 1935). In this Ann Rutherford starring drama, Smiley is a musician, and he contributes with "Deep Dark River" and "What I Wouldn't Do."

THE SINGING VAGABOND (Republic, 1936). Smiley is a saddle pal to U. S. Army Captain Tex Autry, an 1860 period B-Western. This was Gene's only name change while at Republic in any film. On the Western prairies, Burnette has a steady female companion — showgirl Barbara Pepper, who was his first on-screen romance. Smiley comes to Autry's aid in helping rout treacherous Indians and white renegades led by Allan Sears who attack wagon trains of new settlers. Burnette warbles with "Singing Vagabonds" and "Honeymoon Trail."

(Longtime character actor William Frawley, who portrayed cantankerous landlord Fred Mertz on the "I Love Lucy" CBS-TV show during the 1950s, has a brief, unbilled role at start of THE SINGING VAGABOND as a black-face minstrel.)

RED RIVER VALLEY (Republic,1936). TV title with MCA logo is "Man of the Frontier." Smiley ditch rides with pal Gene Autry after saboteurs who attempt wreckage of a dam project using endless dynamite. A mysterious chief ramrods the underhanded operation led by sneaks George Chesebro and Boothe Howard. Burnette has one funny time "teaching" Chesebro the game of checkers, and warbles "Fetch Me Down My Trusty .45." Besides being shot in one scene, Smiley also has a difficult time wrestling a steer, fails to arm wrestle a smaller citizen, and becomes scared at seeing planted dynamite as well as being stomach-punched by player Charles King.

(Note: The film acquired the title MAN OF THE FRONTIER, when it was sold to television to keep the TV bookers from confusing it with the 1941 Roy Rogers movie, RED RIVER VALLEY.)

COMIN' 'ROUND THE MOUNTAIN (Republic,1936). A humorous cowhand on actress Ann Rutherford's horse spread that's involved in chasing down a wild steed, Smiley grabs a number of lengthy riding scenes at Lone Pine, California. He assists Pony Express rider Gene Autry, who confronts fellow rancher LeRoy Mason being after the Rutherford property. The maverick horse El Diablo takes a bite of Burnette's pants seat, and he drinks bottled milk intended for a calf, but Smiley squeezes in time to chant on "Don Juan of Sevillio" and "When the Campfire Is Low On the Prairie." An extra segment allows Smiley also to run into a donkey on the Republic backlot and to pretend as a matador, then later he inadvertently shoots a chicken while target practicing. In the last segment of a horse race, Burnette is roped off his mount only to return by mistake to the starting point.

THE SINGING COWBOY (Republic,1936). Precocious little Ann Gillis suffers a serious back injury when trampled by stampeded horses once her late-murdered father's ranch partner Lon Chaney, Jr. sets a barn fire because of an unknown

gold mine on the property. Such an incident spurs foreman Gene Autry to pay for the Gillis surgery by organizing Burnette and other cowhands into Gene Autry's Television Troubadours. Smiley relies too much on horseshoes for luck only to learn they bring him bad luck such as a bump on the head and being towed by a milk cow. Burnette has his face smeared, too, with a shaving brush full of lather by female lead Lois Wilde. There are noticeably big 40-inch TV sets, or even larger ones, here as Smiley is limited to the songs "Ya-Hoo," "Down in Slumberland," and "The New Jassackaphone."

GUNS AND GUITARS (Republic, 1936). Smiley trudges along with original comedy in this great B-Western as a medicine-show trouper who saddles alongside pal Gene Autry while hunting for whoever attempted the killing of sheriff Jack Rockwell and slew deputy Ken Cooper. The perpetrators are crooked cattle association head J. P. McGowan and rancher Tom London wanting to ship diseased stock infected with Texas cattle fever. A very funny scene of some length has Burnette putting up a sheriff's election poster but interfered with by bad guy Charles King who slaps Smiley with paste. Smiley does a laugh-filled, hip-wiggling dance and mind-reading act as a veiled princess being spurred on by funnyman Earle Hodgins along with running on bare ground not wearing any shoes and has a pitcher of water poured on him by Autry. Burnette contributes his accordian and/or vocal talents to "I've Got Fine Relations" plus "Guns and Guitars."

THE BORDER PATROLMAN (20th Century-Fox, 1936). In mid-May 1936 while Gene Autry was beginning a 60-day pay strike against Republic, Smiley Burnette was probably loaned out—if that were the case—by Republic to work with star George O'Brien for this B-Western as his pal Chuck Owens. It was the only time Smiley worked at another movie studio while under contract to Republic. His song contributions were "Take Me Back to My Boots and Saddle," "Frog Song," and "El Rancho Grande."

OH, SUSANNA! (Republic, 1936). With Gene Autry off his first Republic dispute, Burnette goes in front of studio cameras again with Gene, but mainly confines his screen activities and accompanying loudmouth thespian Earle Hodgins. Smiley and Earle are part of a two-man comic team traveling together who connect up with Autry to help him chase down escaped convict/murderer Boothe Howard. Burnette's funny moments include not getting a decent meal in jail, falling off his horse attempting a stand, dressing as a woman while he and Hodgins warble "They Never Come Through With the Ring," and has knives thrown at him by Earle who pretends drunkenness. A fast-moving B-vehicle for Smiley who also sings "Oh, Susanna." (Ouch! One critic wrote of Gene's OH, SUSANNA! performance, "Autry is as unemotional as a log".)

RIDE RANGER RIDE (Republic, 1936). Here, Smiley's wearing a big, wide, and floppy-brimmed black hat which was to be so much a part of his Frog Millhouse character. Burnette returns to the Old West as an enlisted U. S. Army trooper with Lieut. Gene Autry after both depart the Texas Rangers upon this organization's temporary demise. No sooner have they settled into their new jobs than Gene and Smiley have to battle treacherous Indians led by renegade Monte Blue, in hiding as a saloon proprietor. This feature was comedian/ventriloquist Max Terhune's film debut with Terhune saddling more than Smiley next to Gene. Burnette engages in a continual running gag literally to flee Chief Thundercloud who wants his scalp. Smiley sneezes uncontrollably anytime Terhune uses snuff, but, during a saloon brawl, Burnette saves Autry from being knifed in the back by Blue. Once Gene is kicked out of the Army for supposedly shooting a redskin in an unwarranted manner, Smiley and Max, along with other troopers, start a fracas in Monte Blue's establishment to be deliberately expelled as well. Events, however, change later for both Autry and Burnette when Smiley brings in the Rangers to save settlers from a final Indian raid. Burnette participates with group singing of the title song on horseback and a repititious chorus of "Marche Militaire" in jail next to Autry and Terhune as well as "The Bugle

Song." These tunes limit Smiley's vocals.

THE BIG SHOW (Republic, 1936). Burnette makes his longest location trek to date outside California with star Gene Autry as they arrive in Dallas, Texas for acting participation during The Texas Centennial in 1936. Rest of this movie was lensed back on The Golden State's turf. Smiley partners with Autry who has to assume personal appearance duties during the Centennial as replacement for his snobbish Western star whom he doubles in action movies. Burnette has to compete for song time here with this oatuner's four other music groups that include The Sons of the Pioneers. Funny moments keeping Smiley occupied are a fire started under the chair he's seated on, chasing after Autry's horse Champion, pulling a rickshaw into a lagoon, falling off a camera truck while asleep, being tricked by a "talking" horse, attempting to be a stuntman, and tugging on the tail of a steer moving fast. Burnette helps croon "The Martins and the Coys," "I'm Mad About You," "Wild and Wooley West," and "Nobody's Darlin' But Mine."

(Much of the movie was filmed in Dallas at the 1936 Texas Centennial site, which is now the fairgrounds for the Texas State Fair. Many of the buildings still exist.)

(Dual roles were quite common in B-Westerns. Gene, Roy Rogers and several other B-western performers did them. See the section on Dual Roles.)

THE OLD CORRAL (Republic, 1936). Burnette is deputy sheriff to lawman Gene Autry who corrals Chicago gangster John Bradford threatening the life of songstress Hope Manning having witnessed a mob murder. Smiley gets into more predicaments by jamming his hand in a jail lock, not being able to find his holster gun, fending off Bradford's gunmen while protecting Manning, plus has problems continually transferring on horseback to other mounts. Burnette warbles just "Five Man Band," a very weak tune that causes jailbird Jim Corey to remark: "I thought it was terrible."

(Gene and Roy, the latter still Leonard Slye with The Sons of the Pioneers in his early film career, have a battle and, since it is an Autry movie, Gene is the winner.)

OTHER SMILEY FILMS OF 1936

UNDERSEA KINGDOM (Republic, 1936). When Republic Studios learned that Universal was producing their Flash Gordon serial, they rushed this serial, using similar plot elements, into production. Ray "Crash" Corrigan was the star. Smiley has the great character name of Briny Deep.

HEARTS IN BONDAGE (Republic, 1936). Smiley is barely noticeable as a character called Rammer in this Mae Clarke and James Dunn starring film.

A MAN BETRAYED (Republic, 1936). The movie features Lloyd Hughes, Carleton Young and Edward Nugent. Smiley is billed as "Hillbilly."

DOUGHNUTS AND SOCIETY (A Mascot production released by Republic, 1936). Look fast or you won't see Smiley here as he appears briefly as one of the movers. The picture starred Louise Fazenda and Maude Eburne.

ROUND-UP TIME IN TEXAS (Republic, 1937). Starts out on a good premise with horse rancher Gene Autry leaving Texas to search for missing brother Ken Cooper, having discovered a diamond mine in South Africa. But the picture's screenplay soon disintegrates into a pretty sorry spectacle, and Burnette is partly responsible dressing up in black face, plus sarong, along with African singers be-bopping too much. Plot then stumbles for the film's remaining time. But there are a couple of funny scenes for Smiley that include drinking magic liquid that blows flame after lighting a match and swallowing a small harmonica with him playing a tune when Burnette's stomach is pressed. Burnette, as well, confronts both a gorilla and lion in the same segment, and is arrested for illicit diamond smuggling with Autry, later escaping on their horses from the police. Smiley also comes to Autry's side in rescuing Cooper from kidnapper LeRoy Mason, and contributes to "When the Bloom Is On the Sage," "The Old Chisholm Trail," "Uncle Noah's Ark," "Voice Improvisation," "Cave Man," and "Dinah."

(This is an off-beat Autry/Burnette movie — not appreciated by many. Smiley provides some laughs — sometimes in black face. Stock footage of ferocious animals from "Darkest Africa" (Republic serial, 1936) is added for excitement. Ray "Crash" Corrigan appears in his gorilla suit.)

GIT ALONG LITTLE DOGIES (Republic, 1937). Cattle rancher Gene Autry has his hands full trying to match tit-for-tat with female wildcat and radio personality Judith Allen over an oil well's impending gusher because of Gene's concerns on pollution of water sources. But Smiley Burnette prefers remaining on the sidelines to chase/capture butterflies for a living instead of earnings as a cowhand as Gene goes after oil-well-leaser Weldon Heyburn who wants such profits for himself. More Burnette comedy includes talking to a live frog in Kern River, and jumping inadvertently into Lake Sherwood as well as slamming a pistol onto his fingers. Smiley sings and/or accompanies on "Git Along Little Dogies," "Honey, Bringing Honey to You," Chinatown," and "If You Want to Be a Cowboy."

(The picture features an audience sing-along with the words of six tunes flashed on the screen.)

ROOTIN' TOOTIN' RHYTHM (Republic, 1937). Burnette does much saddle time for this good and quick-moving B-Western as he and pal Gene Autry hunt for cattle rustlers guided by crooked cattle association bigwig Monte Blue whose orders resulted in a raid on ranch stock he shares with co-owner Hal Taliaferro. Smiley resists his nemeses by blowing sneeze powder into their faces as part of a constant bag of tricks. Smiley and Gene also are mistaken for wanted desperadoes Charles King and Max Hoffman Jr. Burnette ropes the gun from Hoffman's hand at the end of an exciting chase and croons on or assists with "The Old Home Place," "Little Black Bronc," and "Dying Cowgirl," the latter which Smiley warbles very badly nearly falling asleep.

Memorable dialogue (Gene and Frog enter a bar pretending to be murderous outlaws):
Bartender: "What'll you have, strangers?"
Frog: "I'd like a glass of milk."
Gene (elbows Frog): "Aw, he's always kidding. We drink whiskey straight and wash it down with lye."

YODELIN' KID FROM PINE RIDGE (Republic, 1937). Smiley departs as usual saddle pal for Gene Autry and doesn't wear his Frog outfit, but takes on the role of Colonel Millhouse, rambunctious entrepreneur of a Wild West Show. Burnette, at the end, leads his troupers with Gene to corral cattle thieves led by crooked LeRoy Mason, stirring up ranchers and mountaineers. Smiley contributes "Georgia Rodeo." Of note here is that Burnette sports a mustache. Among the funniness for Smiley are falling in a water trough, having pottery dropped on his head, and firing two guns at escaping rustlers.

(This the only Autry film in which "Millhouse" was not preceded by "Frog.")

PUBLIC COWBOY NO. 1 (Republic, 1937). An exciting Autry outdoor sagebrusher with still more cattle rustling done by fast-moving culprits who use refrigerated truck vans to stash their stolen beef. Burnette gets more film time for comedy as a deputy sheriff helping head deputy Gene and sheriff William Farnum bring in gang leader Arthur Loft. He and Autry friend Frankie Marvin dress in a cowhide outfit to blend in with other cattle, only the disguise backfires once a bull chases them. Then there's the freezing time Burnette spends locked up in one of Loft's vans with slaughtered meat. Smiley lends his voice to "Heebie Jeebie Blues" driving actor House Peters Jr. bats and "Defective Detective From Brooklyn" and plays the harmonica for "The West Ain't What It Used to Be."

(The cowsuit gimmick also appears in the Roy Rogers film HEART OF THE GOLDEN WEST (Republic, 1942), but this time it is Smiley and Gabby Hayes in the cow outfit.)

BOOTS AND SADDLES (Republic, 1937). There's plenty of activity here for Smiley Burnette as he sides with foreman Gene Autry in keeping an English lad's spread from being taken over by crooked fellow rancher Gordon Elliott. Burnette races a buckboard standing up only to fall to the ground, dances to a Mexican tune after which he's kicked by a jackass, blows continuously on an Army bugle, runs fast on command of a parrot, is fired at by a machine gun, drills on command of player Stanley Blystone, rides with Autry to rope horses for an Army race to save young Ra Hould's due mortgage payment to Elliott, plus bicycles to capture arsonist Bud Osborne on Lone Pine turf. Sings "Dusty Roads" riding backwards on his ungroomed white horse and helps on "Ridin' the Range," and "Take Me Back to My Boots and Saddle."

SPRINGTIME IN THE ROCKIES (Republic, 1937). Burnette goes through a tedious process with cattle ranch foreman Gene Autry while attempting to persuade spread owner Polly Rowles that she shouldn't raise sheep on the property that's strictly part of cattle country. Smiley is complicit with Autry in scaring Rowles and her girlfriends doing his wild animal noises as well as using a tow truck on jail-bar windows to enable Gene's escape from jail in one scene. Rowles does not know it, but she's played into the hands of schemers Alan Bridge and Edward Hearn wanting her ranch to raise woolies. Burnette warbles "Way Down Low," "Down In the Land of Zulu," and provides accompaniment on "Give Me a Pony" and "When It's Springtime In the Rockies."

Memorable dialogue (The new owner has just shipped dozens of equipment crates to the ranch):
Frog: "Well, I'll be hung for a horse thief — soil testing equipment, encyclopedias, and chemicals and poison — well, who in blazes sent all that junk out here?"
Gene: "That's easy, our lady boss. She's going to an agricultural college and taking up animal husbandry."
Frog: "Husbandry, huh? Well, it do beat all what women will do to get married."

OTHER SMILEY FILMS OF 1937

MANHATTAN MERRY-GO-ROUND (Republic, 1937). The film stars Phil Regan and Leo Carrillo. Smiley plays Frog the accordion player. Baseball great Joe DiMaggio has a small role. There is a lot of wasted talent in this terrible movie. Helps Gene Autry sing "It's Round-up Time in Reno."

DICK TRACY (Republic, 1937). This is a Ralph Byrd starring serial. Smiley plays a character called Mike McGurk in this 15-chapter serial, and it is not one of his better performances.

LARCENY ON THE AIR (Republic, 1937). In this Robert Livingston non-Western, Smiley is called Jimmy. Livingston, of *The Three Mesquiteers* fame, is a crusading young doctor out to smash the influence of quack doctors. The leading lady is Grace Bradley, who married William "Hopalong Cassidy" Boyd this same year.

MEET THE BOY FRIEND (Republic, 1937). Smiley leads an orchestra in this Carol Hughes and David Carlyle (Robert Paige) feature.

THE OLD BARN DANCE (Republic, 1938). Truly one wonderful Gene Autry B-Western before the movie cowboy went on a five-month Republic pay strike, Smiley abets the fast-moving theme of him and Gene wanting to sell their horses to farmers instead of the latter group purchasing tractors from the firm of crooked Ivan Miller. Burnette joins Autry hunting down horse thieves and frees mechanical mice to interfere with tractor sales among other hilarious segments. He also endures the melee of two big fight scenes where there were an unusual amount of player injuries. Smiley warbles on "Ten Little Miles," "Old Nell," and "Listen to the Mockingbird," and plays "At the Old Barn Dance" on his jassackaphone.

UNDER WESTERN STARS (Republic, 1938). While Autry was striking against Republic, Smiley became cast by the studio into new B-cowboy star Roy Rogers' 1st lead film still as Frog Millhouse. Burnette ably assists Rogers, as a Congressman, in obtaining the water bill for drought-stricken ranchers. Smiley introduces Black-Eyed Nellie, now his official screen horse, the white steed with a painted black circle around its left eye. Burnette has numerous side-splitting moments as Nellie, a fire horse, reacts everytime a bell is rung compelling the crazy animal to set out on a running rampage. Nellie is even ridden by actor Dick Elliott as the Congressman who loses his re-election to Rogers. More funny times for Smiley have him dropping a valve wheel into Tinemaha Dam, stopping the dam guards from shooting Rogers, dressing in riding clothes for a fox hunt at Lake Sherwood whereupon he's forced up a tree by numerous hound dogs, humorously kidding water company executive Kenneth Harlan, and pulling down a town hall bell covered with dust. Smiley contributes with "Send My Mail to the County Jail," "Vote for Rogers," and "Back to the Back Woods." After this hard-riding feature, Burnette went touring

cross country to promote it with Rogers.

(Roy, Smiley and The Sons of the Pioneers were at the film's premiere in Dallas, Texas during April 1938 for a stage show prior to the picture.)

GOLD MINE IN THE SKY (Republic, 1938). Gene Autry's now off strike, and he and Smiley Burnette reunite in hell-bent-for-leather riding footage and excellent tunes, plus great comedy that make this Autry oatuner his very best for Republic. Burnette establishes the Frog Millhouse black-hat style permanently here for the remainder of his B-Western career by folding straight up the chapean's front brim. Gene's got a plateful of trouble with ranch heiress Carol Hughes as her foreman while curtailing rustling of property cattle by Hughes' fiancé Craig Reynolds and cohorts LeRoy Mason and Eddie Cherkose. Smiley dons plump actress Cupid Ainsworth's clothes to fool Reynolds who has demanded $25,000 ransom to save Hughes' life. At end of this movie, Ainsworth wears Burnette's outfit with Smiley riding off in great disbelief. Burnette accompanies with "Hummin' When We're Comin' Round the Bend," "That's How Donkeys Were Born," "Dude Ranch Cowhands," "Hike Yaa," and "Tumbleweed Tenor."

(J. L. Frank, the promoter who introduced Gene and Smiley in 1933, got his son-in-law Pee Wee King and His Golden West Cowboys a part in this film.)

MAN FROM MUSIC MOUNTAIN (Republic, 1938). Smiley, desiring not to be just an Autry cowhand forever, opens an electrical gadget store on the promise that water/power via Boulder Dam are coming to the once ghost town of Gold River. He and Gene have to encounter phony realtors Ivan Miller and Edward Cassidy as Burnette has one uproarious scene when all his gadgets go amok after electricity is functional. Some of the other hilarity done by Smiley includes becoming soused on sasparilla with a barroom scene where bartender Hal Price

spikes his drink with gin. He is also snookered with a phony character analysis by con man Earle Hodgins. Smiley's tricked purchase of stock shares in the local mine that eventually pays off after a new gold vein is discovered finds Burnette more business savvy than Autry himself here. The comic warbles on "Man From Music Mountain," "Love, Burning Love," where he razzes Gene in a beauty parlor, "All Nice People," and "She Works Third Tub At the Laundry."

BILLY THE KID RETURNS (Republic, 1938). Burnette is a musical instrument peddler here in his 2nd B-Western as sidekick to Roy Rogers who has a dual role also as Billy the Kid against New Mexico territorial horse rustlers. Smiley becomes very funny while palming off instruments on outlaws Fred Kohler Sr. and Morgan Wallace. Burnette assists on "Sing a Little Song About Anything," "We're the Dixie Brand" and "The Dixie Instruments Song." At this point in his Republic acting career, Smiley Burnette complained to the studio about being over burdened with film work since 1935. After all, besides the Autrys, Burnette had also acted in 11 other films, which included two 1936 and 1937 Republic serials. Satisfied with his current salary, he reached an understanding with Republic to only appear in future Gene Autry oatuners.

Memorable dialogue: Frog: "Why you are Roy Rogers. I use to go to school with him down in Texas; I was in the third grade nine years down there."

PRAIRIE MOON (Republic, 1938). Smiley has his hands full trying to tame, along with deputy sheriff Gene Autry's assistance, three young Chicago toughs who have inherited their late gangster father William Pawley's ranch out West. The property is now in Gene's executor hands until the teenagers reach legal age. Unbeknownst to anyone is the fact that sneaky storekeeper Stanley Andrews is using a hidden cave behind waterfalls on the ranch where his gang hides stolen cattle. A couple of scenes where Burnette is aggravated with the kids

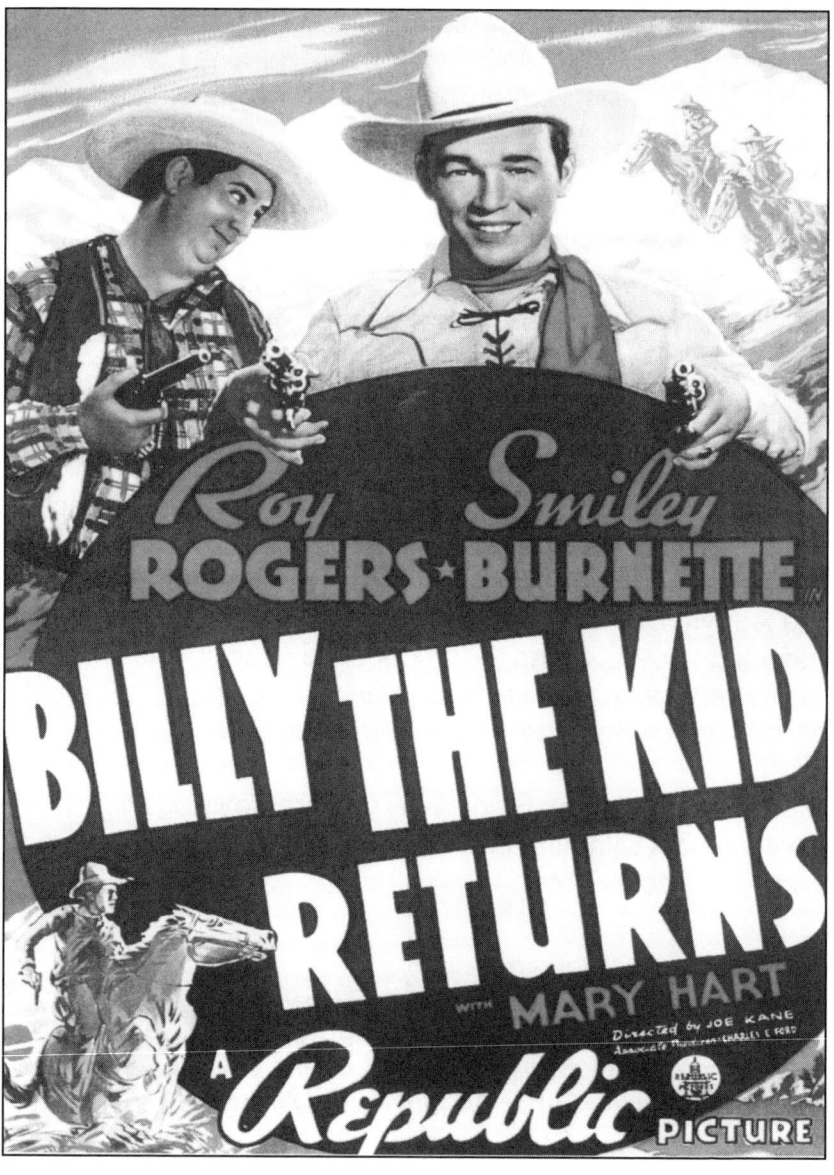

occur when a water bag is dropped on his head, and they tie him to a stake followed by a quickly burning blaze in their bedroom. The boys also cause an earlier buckboard runaway, tripping up Burnette even more and causing him to furiously run after the vehicle. Crossing a creek, he trips and falls into the water. Smiley offers vocals on "Rhythm of the Hoofbeats," "In the Jailhouse Now," and "Story of Trigger Joe."

RHYTHM OF THE SADDLE (Republic, 1938). Smiley Burnette plays up to actress Pert Kelton with whom he desires marriage, but gets cold feet almost at the end of this B-Western musical. He and manager Gene battle crooked nightclub owner LeRoy Mason who craves take over of an annual rodeo franchise, but Smiley trips up the miscreant and pal Arthur Loft with secret recordings. Burnette gets fun time when he dresses in a horse outfit, not being adept at stopping a runaway carriage, etc. On the serious side, Burnette helps Autry rescue horses from a barn fire ignited by bad guy Al Taylor. Smiley warbles with "She'll Be Comin' 'Round the Mountain," "Oh, Ladies," "The Old Trail," and "Let Me Call You Sweetheart."

(Pert Kelton was the original Alice Kramden on TV's "The Honeymooners" (1952).)

WESTERN JAMBOREE (Republic, 1938). Less action than usual for a Gene Autry movie, Smiley Burnette helps the western star rout helium thieves after a precious supply on the ranch where they're employed. They discover old-timer Frank Darien who has lied to daughter Jean Rouverol about his ownership of such property. Autry and Burnette allow Darien to pretend he's the proprietor to impress Rouverol with Smiley later disguised as a wild Indian and bulldogged by Gene to delay her arrival at the ranch. He and comic Joe Frisco hogtie the new owner of the ranch to prevent him from learning anything. Another funny incident has Burnette shot out of the air by Gene while hanging onto a helium-filled balloon. Additional ones have Smiley falling off a fence and letting two intruders escape. Burnette lends his vocals on "Cielito Lindo," "Balloon Song," and "I Love the Morning."

(Look fast and you will spot Eddie Dean briefly as an Autry cowhand.)

OTHER SMILEY FILM OF 1938

HOLLYWOOD STADIUM MYSTERY! (Republic, 1938). Smiley portrays himself for the B-drama.

HOME ON THE PRAIRIE (Republic, 1939). Smiley joins pal Gene Autry with both as livestock inspectors trying hard to prevent hoof-and-mouth disease from spreading while underhanded ranch owner Walter Miller wants to ship his infected cattle in cahoots with crooked stock broker Gordon Hart. While the screenplay contains plenty of mystery and fisticuffs, plus the usual hard-riding action, Smiley gets mixed up with an elephant which he has to push and shove ever so often. The pachyderm is scared by a little terrier which enables Miller and his cohorts to get their cattle-loaded trucks by Burnette in one scene. Then Burnette has to fend off homely/skinny actress Helen Servis at a barn dance. Smiley warbles "There's Nothing Like Work," falling half asleep, but is awakened almost immediately by remedy salesman Earle Hodgins. Does a "Punch and Judy" act with Autry to escape cohorts holding them as prisoners. Later, Smiley uses the elephant to break himself, Autry, and Hodgins from jail.

MEXICALI ROSE (Republic, 1939). This is an especially energetic Autry feature with great music scoring where Burnette rides plenty with broadcast singer Gene to drop evidence on big-time radio-station head William Royle, who craves revenue from leased mission land to pawn off fake shares of stock for a phony oil derrick. If oil is actually discovered, he wants all profit for himself with nothing returned to the mission. Smiley's side-splitting humor includes an oil machine that screams, tripping over a cactus, running blindfolded into a sound-stage tree, letting oil engineer LeRoy Mason flee, and clunking badman Eddie Parker from behind with a wrench. Smiley enthusiastically warbles "My Orchestra's Driving Me Crazy," and "El Rancho Grande."

BLUE MONTANA SKIES (Republic, 1939). After Gene's elder partner Tully Marshall is knifed to death by fur smugglers during a cattle drive, Burnette aids Autry in tracking their illegal operation to nearby dude ranch. Both discover that June Storey partner Harry Woods ramrods this across-the-border set-up between Montana and Canada, which later has Burnette detained, then fleeing during a storage-room blaze to help Gene capture the smugglers. Smiley thoroughly rehearsed the comic footage he had with young juvenile actor Robert Winkler, the biggest segment where Burnette is an Indian chief, and Winkler attempts to drive a nail into the back of his head. Burnette also has to endure knives heaved at him by Winkler's mother, Dorothy Granger, while in a knight's uniform. Granger also pummels Burnette who had earlier accosted Winkler, later handcuffing Smiley while napping. Smiley assists Gene Autry on "Rockin' In the Saddle" and "Old Geezer."

(Smiley created a lot of fun on the set, often causing some retakes, by referring to the fur smugglers as "smur fugglers." June Storey said the performers were sometimes so hysterical that it was difficult to control the laughter so that filming could continue.)

MOUNTAIN RHYTHM (Republic, 1939). Smiley sees that his aunt Maude Eburne keeps her ranch along with properties of other owners from being seized at public action by unscrupulous businessman Walter Fenner who desperately needs their lands for a vast health center. Burnette and pal Gene Autry, have humorous footage after pilfering architect plans for this new center upon their chase from Fenner's office with help of his resort employees around hallways that takes on the air of a Three Stooges comedy short. Smiley practices hypnotism on lawman Slim Whitaker, and is pulled off his horse by a badly misplaced rope across a road to trap pursuers among other of his comic feats here. Burnette lends his voice on "Highways Are Happy Ways," "It Makes No Difference Now," "It Was Only a Hobo's Dream," "Old MacDonald," "Old Gray Mare," "Long, Long Ago," "Oh Dem Golden Slippers," and "Put On Your Old Gray Bonnet."

(talking about the rickety wagon driven by Burnette):
Gene: "Boy, you'll be lucky if this thing holds together till we get to Pueblo City."
Frog: "Well, don't worry about it. It came all the way from Texas, didn't it? I ain't walked yet!"

COLORADO SUNSET (Republic, 1939). Smiley Burnette has active romance with café owner Barbara Pepper while he and partner Gene Autry lock horns against crooked veterinarian Robert Barrat. It seems the latter is trying to force dairy farmers into joining his protection racket or face having their milk supplies destroyed by night-riding gunmen. Smiley does full-time duty accompanying Gene against deputy sheriff Buster Crabbe for election to the sheriff's post vacated upon William Farnum's murder by Barrat. Burnette isn't too successful at milking cows and marches against rowdies Ethan Laidlaw and Bill Yrigoyen as they fail in putting up unwanted Crabbe election posters. But the funniest time for Smiley comes as he sabotages Crabbe's rally by speaking negatives about Gene's opponent into a microphone on a rapid basis, and later lures the Barrat gang into a shootout. Burnette croons "On My Merry Old Way Back Home," "Cowboys Don't Milk Cows," "Beautiful Isle of Somewhere," and "Autry's Your Man."

(Western music icon Patsy Montana sings "I Want to Be a Cowboy's Sweetheart." The song has been cut from most copies of the movie. Elmo Lincoln, the screen's first Tarzan,

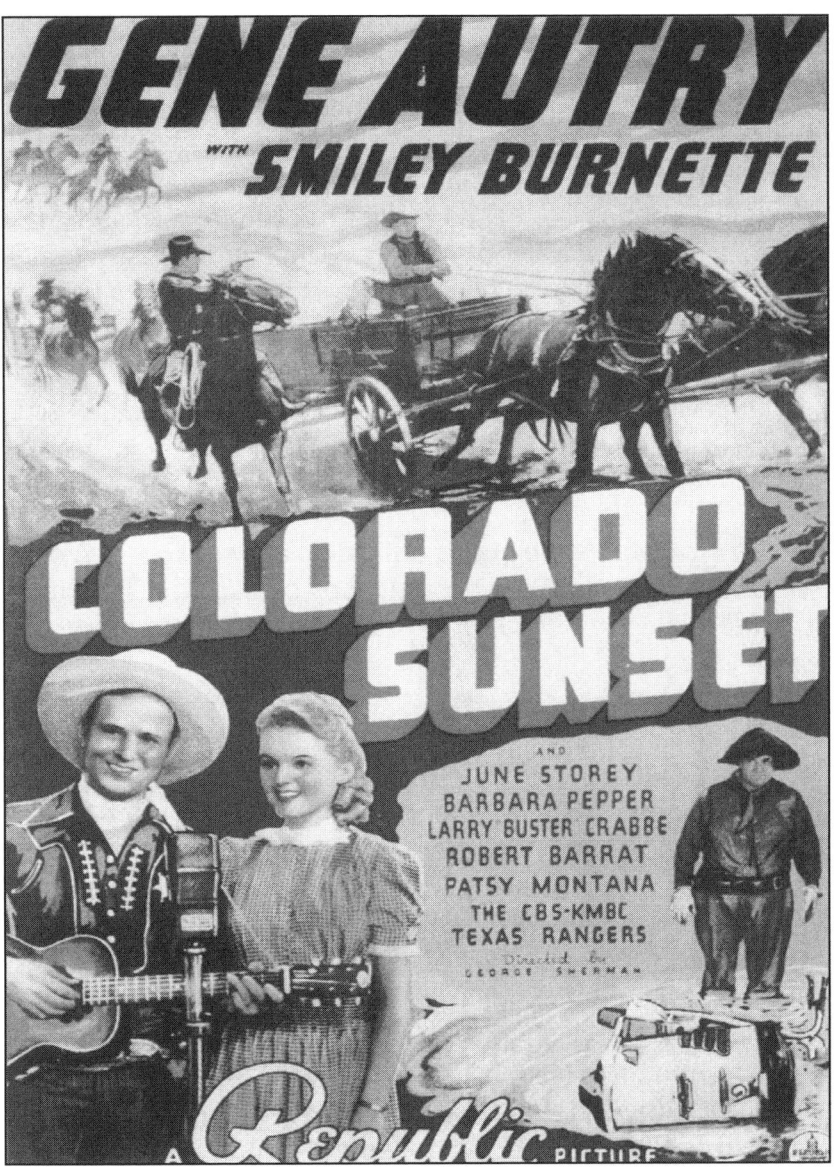

has a small part in the picture.)

IN OLD MONTEREY (Republic, 1939). This Gene Autry B-Western has Smiley joining his saddle pal sergeant as a U. S. Army deserter to secure ranch acreage, opposed by current occupants, for a bombing range. Taking on its patriotic war theme during 1939 with battles raging in East Asia and Eastern Europe, this movie is greatly sidetracked for Burnette by too much foolishness from The Hoosier Hot Shots musicians who waste screen time with horseplay and their crude instruments. He also has to share footage with Roy Rogers' sidekick George "Gabby" Hayes. Some of the antics have Smiley steering an Army tank, being chased onto an active Army bombing strip on horseback, wrecking a nightclub, and accidentally jumping from a window into a water barrel. Burnette sings "It Looks Like Rain" and "Skeleton Rag."

(When Frog and Gene grab a tank to go after the borax crooks Jonathan Hale and William Hall, Gabby gets to ride Champion. It is interesting that the movie was set in 1939 and made that same year.)

ROVIN' TUMBLEWEEDS (Republic, 1939). Burnette travels to Washington, DC with Congressman Gene Autry for the purpose of obtaining a flood-control bill for their water-ravaged constituents. Gene's attempts are blocked by greedy developer Douglass Dumbrille who craves ranchers lands just for the taxes owed. Burnette also helps Autry attack blockers of flood refugees from coming into a dry county and is jumped on by numerous school kids, one of whom pelts him with a tomato. Smiley contributes on "Ole Peaceful River," "Away Out Yonder," "On the Sunny Side of the Cell," "Rocky Mountain Express," and "Hurray." FLASH NEWS: George "Gabby" Hayes, clean-shaven and having no long hair, stands next to a radio as Gene sings "Back In the Saddle Again."

SOUTH OF THE BORDER (Republic, 1939). Smiley Burnette's in love again—this time with Autry leading lady June Storey, but differing circumstances and events always interfere in his romance of her, including horse Black-Eyed Nellie. Smiley and Gene are federal agents who stop foreign infiltrators from establishing a refueling base for submarines on Pan American territory. Smiley saddles with Autry to stop a runaway carriage hauling actress Lupita Tovar, then assists Gene in setting up a rendezvous so he can romance her. Burnette is punched, as well, by teenager Mary Lee, and drives cattle to the Pacific Ocean. Cantina girl Sheila Darcy flirts with Burnette who has to fend off threat of knifing from steady beau Dick Botiller. Smiley warbles with "Come to the Fiesta," "Fat Caballero," "Girl of My Dreams," "When the Cactus Blooms Again," and "South of the Border."

RANCHO GRANDE (Republic, 1940). Smiley, along with Autry and the rest of this cast, have a wonderful time doing robust songs making this B-Western musical an all-around top Gene Autry feature. Burnette has funny episodes as he aids Gene in taming three young inheritors — June Storey, Dick Hogan, and Mary Lee — from being fleeced of a vast rancho by unscrupulous attorney Ferris Taylor. Burnette is kidded by Mary Lee using a microphone into thinking he's gone crazy, and he has a bad experience with heavy car exhaust furmes. Smiley also has aid from a donkey to escape marriage from man-crazy society columnist Ellen Lowe when she runs into the small animal and creates other hilarious moments with her, then goes at it in a big nightclub melee. Burnette goes into a lively mood while contributing to "El Rancho Grande," "Dude Ranch Cowhands," and "You Can Take the Boy Out of the Country."

GAUCHO SERENADE (Republic, 1940). Burnette has a full platter of problems controlling runaways June Storey and Mary Lee as they elude the law after Storey abandons a prospective bridegroom. Smiley rescues both girls from Lake Hemet after

A very young Mary Lee (left), in her first Gene Autry picture with SOUTH OF THE BORDER (Republic, 1939), constantly interferes with Smiley Burnette's attempted romance of leading lady June Storey.

Smiley Burnette, Fay McKenzie, and Gene Autry are all smiles for this studio publicity shot on SIERRA SUE (Republic, 1941).

their car plunges into deep water upon speeding too fast. Mixed up in the melee, as well, is pal Gene Autry who also proves the innocence of English lad Clifford Severn Jr.'s father Lester Matthews on phony embezzlement charges at the hand of meat-packing crook Joseph Crehan. Burnette finds himself very scared of a bat flying inside the barn where he and Autry take refuge running comically up against Storey hiding there. Smiley sings on "Headin' For the Wide Open Spaces," "Wooing of Kitty McFooty," and "Keep Rollin'."

(Not much action here. One VARIETY *critic wrote: First horse is not mounted until 44 minutes have passed; first fist is not flung until 50 minutes have passed; first gun is not fired until 56 minutes have passed. What manner of Western is this?)*

CAROLINA MOON (Republic, 1940). Smiley's involved with another woman — it's actress Terry Nibert, but he wants nothing to do with her. Smiley also has to fend off Nibert's father Frank Dae who wants to duel with him on a constant basis in the Deep South. Autry has assurance from Burnette to squelch the plot of greedy plantation owner Hardie Albright to grab other nearby properties for the valuable timber. Smiley is hilarious also as a black-faced mammy, inadvertently greasing Albright's hands, pulling Nibert out of heavy bushes, and helps Dae throw rocks at crooked lumber cutters. He sings with "Carolina Moon," "My Echo and Me," and "At the Rodeo."

RIDE, TENDERFOOT, RIDE (Republic, 1940). Burnette does some of his fastest trotting at Republic here all because of one very tiny terrier which chases him any time Smiley comes close to the animal after he absently leaves a cattle-train door open which allows the stock to flee. The dog, owned by leading lady June Storey, even forces Burnette to dive into a swimming pool. Burnette, in the meantime, upon fainting with one scene, sidekicks with partner Gene Autry who tries to keep his inherited meat-packing outfit from falling into the hands of unscrupulous rival Warren Hull. Smiley accompanies on

"When the Work's All Done This Fall," "Eleven More Months and Ten More Days" and "That Was Me By the Sea." He also has lengthy conversation with clothier Joe Frisco over what suits to purchase and does an awkward dance with actress Lucille Browne.

Memorable dialogue: Gene: "I'd feel a lot more at home down in the stockyard."
Frog: "Well, me too. I-I don't like being cooped up. You're liable to get hydrophobia or something."

RIDIN' ON A RAINBOW (Republic, 1941). Burnette has a humorous time aboard a showboat becoming seasick and falling overboard while he aids Autry in wanting to capture bank robbers Ralf Harolde and Anthony Warde who murdered employee Burr Caruth during the holdup. On the comedy side, Smiley inadvertently turns on a water hose which douses female lead Carol Adams with a liquid flood. Burnette croons and/or accompanies ably with the tunes "Hunky Dunky Dory," "Be Honest With Me," "Steamboat Bill," and "Ridin' On a Rainbow."

BACK IN THE SADDLE (Republic, 1941). Smiley is suppose to keep tabs upon foreman Gene Autry's instructions, on young ranch owner Edward Norris. The latter is slicker than an eel and escapes Burnette's watch a number of times as he and Gene take up the task of battling sneaky Arthur Loft, a saloon owner who operates his copper mine that is poisoning the local river supply of water with sulfate runoff. Smiley becomes tangled with a saddle that he dumps on a suitcase full of clothes, fights rowdies at a chess club, stands on his head to sing a tune, tries talking into a radio mike, has a bird cage smashed against him during a saloon brawl, throws a horseshoe against leading lady Jacqeline Wells' car windsheield, and trips on his own two feet into a birthday cake. Such an array of comic feats still leaves Burnette time to drive cattle into the middle of town with the purpose of ending a raging shootout with Autry

and Norris defending themselves against Loft and the outlaw gang. Burnette croons "Ninety-Nine Bullfrogs," and helps Gene on "You Are My Sunshine."

THE SINGING HILL (Republic, 1941). Smiley Burnette, in true comedic fashion, jumps in with foreman Gene Autry to halt ranch boss Virginia Dale, scatterbrained to the hilt, from selling her property to crooked cattle broker George Meeker. When other cattlemen threaten to storm Gene over their grazing rights possibly being sacrificed on the ranch Gene operates, Smiley keeps them at bay with a perfume bottle thought to actually contain a liquid explosive. And Burnette, with aid of youngster Mary Lee fails in an uproarious manner to cease Dale's man servant Gerald Oliver Smith from babbling about an impending Autry cattle drive with other ranchers to pay off $25,000 to Meeker for the initial option money he turned over for ranch payment to Dale. Smiley tangles with bad guy Jim Corey in a funny fisticuffs segment, but has big trouble subduing his nemesis. Burnette pipes in with "Ridin' Down That Old Texas Trail," "Let a Smile Be Your Umbrella," and "Sail the Seven Seas."

SUNSET IN WYOMING (Republic, 1941). At Autry's side as the ranch owner appeals to big lumber baron George Cleveland not to radically cut down too much timber which is causing big floods from torrential rains, Burnette has plenty of problems himself almost being run over by out-of-control riders and being tossed out of an exclusive club into a cactus patch along with being hit in a car accident by actress Maris Wrixon. Smiley poses as a butler for a big society gathering only to be jailed with Gene, and works with so-called "wild animals" for one scene that backfires. He even throws a pie into the face of an innocent citizen, and assists Gene by tossing crooked lumber foreman Stanley Blystone into a creek for attempted bribery. Smiley sings "I Was Born In Old Wyoming" and "Casey Jones."

UNDER FIESTA STARS (Republic, 1941). Republic, evidently trying something different, brought in young actor Joseph Strauch Jr. to be Smiley's brother Tadpole Millhouse who wore identical clothing to Burnette's character of Frog. But it's wasted screen time with too many silly moments for the pair. Burnette and Strauch beat up on each other and exchange a lot of worthless dialogue; however, Smiley squeezes in some meaningful comedy for himself by falling off a log walkway into lake water with actress Pauline Drake who is taken for a moonlight walk, as well, by Burnette to a hog pen. He also tickles his stomach with a mine drill while partner Gene Autry successfully prevents female lead Carol Hughes from selling half of their mine holdings to shady consultants Ivan Miller and Sam Flint. Smiley also shares his voice with "Man On the Flying Trapeze," and "Keep It In the Family," but plays the accordion as Gene warbles on "I've Got No Use For Women." Burnette joins in a big exchange of gunfire against the mine raiders plus participating in subduing them with fists near the film's end.

DOWN MEXICO WAY (Republic, 1941). Smiley receives comedy competition from actor Harold Huber who portrays reformed Mexican bandit Pancho Grande working as a barbecue cook at Autry's ranch. But it works out marvelously for both comedians in this big-costing Gene Autry "deluxe special" while they come to the cowboy star's side in pursuit of phony movie producers Sidney Blackmer and Arthur Loft between lively musical numbers, and kidnap female lead Fay McKenzie to have her hatch a money plan to capture them. Then both Burnette and Huber are detained by the men they're pursuing only to escape for a wild motorcycle ride. Among Smiley's funny and humorous segments here are throwing a meat cleaver which lands in the side of a convertible door, complaining of being cheated out of $12.84 with worthless movie stock, swallows a tiny musical instrument, and drinking sauce which lights Huber's cigar. Smiley reluctantly, also escorts actress Ruth Robinson, and later wards off ambush from the Blackmer/Loft gang. Burnette boisterously croons on "Beer Barrel Polka" and plays his harmonica for "South of

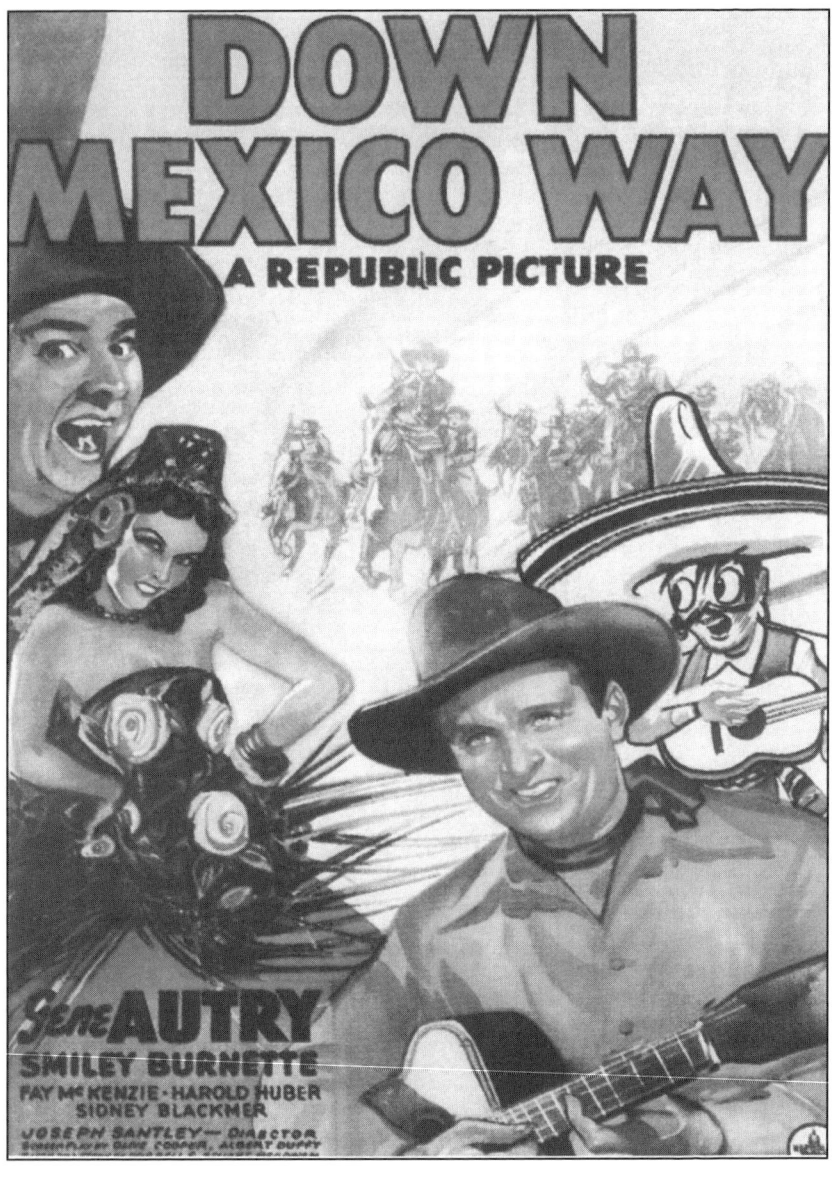

the Border" during his music times.

SIERRA SUE (Republic, 1941). Smiley's heart starts pounding love beats once he sights lovely leading lady Fay McKenzie whom he thinks of marrying, but pal Autry runs end interference in wanting McKenzie for himself. Burnette also has real humor changing Fay's flat tire on her station wagon, and when he's shot out of a cannon only to land in a cactus patch. Then Smiley has to get relief the hard way by having those needles painfully extracted as well as experiencing the aftermath of tear-gas shells fired at him. Burnette also ropes foreman Hugh Prosser to prevent interference of Gene's program of spraying chemicals to eradicate weed growth. As a distraction for his love of McKenzie, Smiley is lured into the arms of fortune teller Dorothy Christy, who is paid for this feat by Autry. Smiley contributes to "Be Honest With Me," "Heebie Jeebie Blues," and "I'll Be True While You're Gone." Along the way there are more amusing scenes, including one where Smiley, on a date with McKenzie, holds several bags of popcorn while eating an ice cream cone. Eddie Dean appears briefly as a pilot downed twice with the aircraft he's flying.

COWBOY SERENADE (Republic, 1942). Burnette continues to gather female problems, this time with elderly spinster Cecil Cunningham giving him orders while she is companion to leading lady Fay McKenzie. Smiley is an expert at cooking slumgullion for rancher Gene Autry who takes out after a slick gang of card sharps having cheated young Rand Brooks out of a train load of cattle. Burnette and Autry encounter gamblers Tristram Coffin and Johnnie Berkes in a new card game, but have to jump off the train when more of the sharpies try to kill them. They later are held by the gang, but flee with Cunningham's help. In one scene, Smiley dresses as the prudish sister of Cunningham to scare away lawmen. A most unusual circumstance for the conclusion of a Gene Autry oatuner finds Burnette corralling Coffin and confederate Ethan Laidlaw with the unexpected aid of Cunningham, who falls into

Smiley's arms after Brooks and fiancée Melinda Leighton wed. Burnette joins on warbling "Cowboy Serenade."

(Another B-Western sidekick, Arkansas "Slim" Andrews, participates in a funny skit with Smiley. Apparently, Smiley thought Andrews was a little too funny because he saw to it that Andrews appeared in no more Autry features.)

Memorable dialogue: Gene: "I think we've met the head man."
Frog: "Who?"
Gene: "Asa Lock."
Frog: "W-why Gene …"
Gene: "Yeah, he's very smooth on the outside ..."
Frog: "Do you reckon he's one of them Dr. Jekylls and Mr. Lock?"

(While Gene got directions to the bad guy's hideout over the phone, Smiley transcribed the conversation.)

Frog: "I got every word. Now look, you go to the, yeah, turn to the right, yeah, over to the, I see, I got it, thanks. You know if we follow this, we're lost before we get started."

HEART OF THE RIO GRANDE (Republic, 1942). Smiley Burnette's in love with leading lady Fay McKenzie again, and again receives competition from foreman Gene Autry as he attempts to draw her to him. Burnette has a funny time, as well, with young Joe Strauch Jr., back with Gene's series after a three-picture absence. Strauch, Smiley's younger brother, plays tricks on Burnette such as putting horse liniment in hair tonic to make his scalp itch which makes Fay cough. Smiley then goes to a horse trough to wet down his hair to cure such discomfort. Smiley croons with "Deep In the Heart of Texas" and "Oh, Woe Is Me."

HOME IN WYOMIN' (Republic, 1942). Smiley and brother Joe Strauch Jr., have more scenes together here as they accompany Autry who routs out the mystery slayer of news reporter Chick Chandler on a dude ranch. Both Burnette and Strauch razz Gene over his difficulty in romancing female support Fay McKenzie. Smiley's other shenanigans include making noise disturbances in a radio control room, getting scared of a bee while a car passenger, trying to cheat Strauch out of money owed him, playing the jassackaphone, chasing house intruders inside the Republic cave set, and joining Autry in pursuit of Chicago gangsters George Douglas, Bud Geary, and Ken Cooper. Smiley lends his voice on "Tweedle-O-Twill" and "Modern Design."

STARDUST ON THE SAGE (Republic, 1942). Supposedly helping saddlemate Gene Autry persuade ranchers that using their money to purchase cattle instead of investing in a hydraulic mining venture, Smiley Burnette actually wants some of the available stock himself. Smiley does a lot of extended riding segments with Gene to expose crooked mine manager Emmett Vogan. Burnette comes to Autry's aid in nabbing payroll bandits George DeNormand, Jerry Jerome, and Bert LeBaron. He contributes to more antics in tangling with Vogan bad guy Roy Barcroft and uses red ink on himself to scare cohort Tom London into a confession. Then Burnette subdues the gang by using a water hose on them. Smiley contributes to "You Are My Sunshine," "Home On the Range," "Wouldn't You Like to Know?" while performing magic tricks, and "Deep In the Heart of Texas," the latter song where words are flashed on-screen.

(Smiley uses the gimmick of turning to the audience and asking them to participate in a song. This was somewhat popular in several short subjects during the 1940s. He also talks to the audience in some of the Sunset Carson movies, which was not appreciated by the Western film purist.)

CALL OF THE CANYON (Republic, 1942). What with all the music done by The Sons of the Pioneers in this B-oatuner,

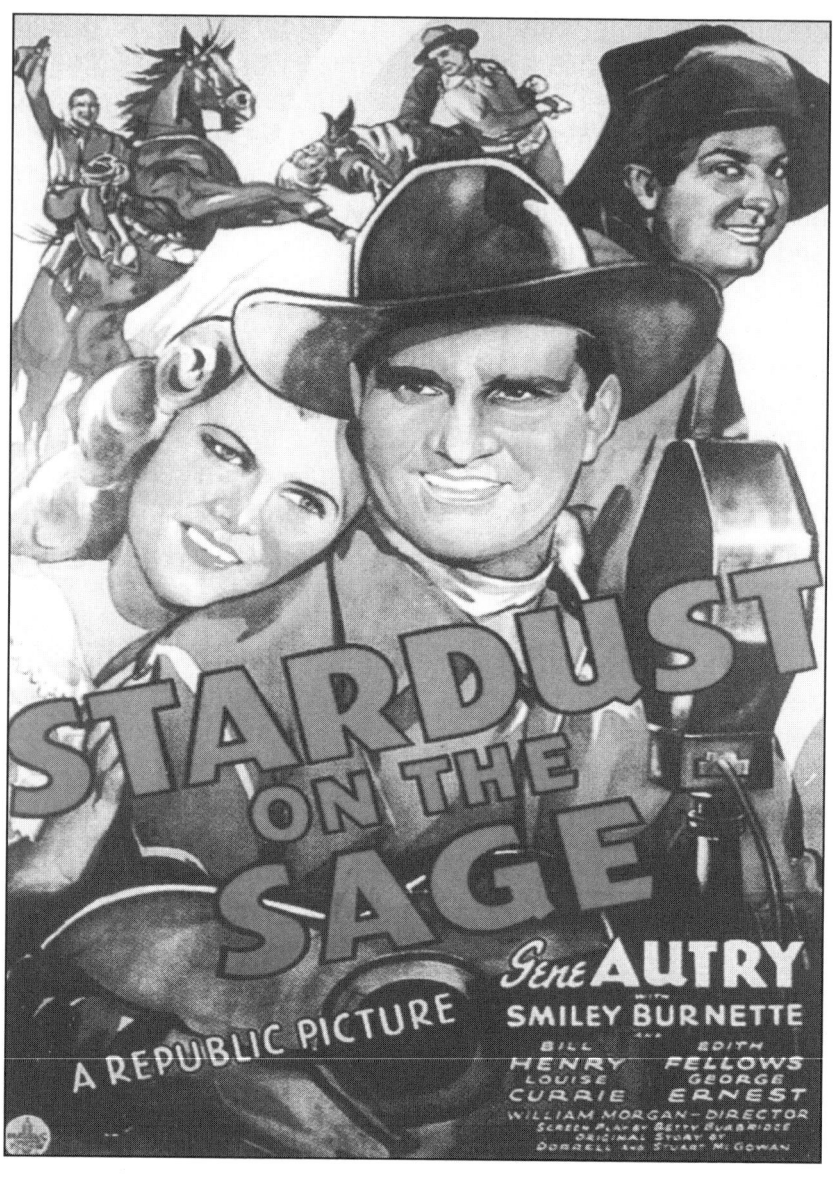

not one song is allotted to Burnette. It's the first time in any Gene Autry feature such a situation happened for Smiley. Instead, he's assigned more to loudly cheer on young brother Joe "Tadpole" Strauch Jr. to win the annual pie-eating contest which the youngster loses. Burnette then, underhandedly, rents Gene's ranch to radio entertainer Ruth Terry for $200 to pay off lost bets for Strauch's failed competition. Smiley also steps into the frey with Gene to defeat crooked cattle packing company agent Edmund MacDonald while herding stock. He and Strauch gave actor Thurston Hall a vigorous rubdown.

(Tadpole looks, acts, and talks like Frog. Although he and Frog often do not get along, when Tadpole is injured in an explosion, Frog sits up with him in one of Gene's house bedrooms. So the viewer knows they are really as close as if they were father and son.)

BELLS OF CAPISTRANO (Republic, 1942). This was goodbye for Smiley Burnette in Gene Autry horse operas at Republic once the cowboy movie star finished emoting here. Autry entered World War II military service on July 26, 1942. He and Smiley would not do any more screen acting together again until another 8 years, 4-1/2 months had elapsed. Burnette accompanies on guitar while Autry croons "Fort Worth Jail," and does no singing whatsoever. His part here is very limited, but Smiley has a paint brush thrown in his face during a fight and eats a rare meal while jailed plus frees corraled horses at the outset of a rodeo blaze. Burnette participates in a big saloon scuffle with rodeo big shot Morgan Conway and his gang wanting rival Virginia Grey's enterprise. Grey turns in an outstanding performance.

HEART OF THE GOLDEN WEST (Republic, 1942). Smiley was cast into this Roy Rogers B-musical feature 40 days after completing Gene Autry's last starring Republic B-Western at the time. A movie full of action, comedy, and tunes, it should have been a natural for Burnette, still as Frog Millhouse, but he was shoved aside with only a paucity of camera appearances during Roy's dealings against scheming cattle shipper Edmund MacDonald. A majority of funniness though is handled by extra sidekicks George "Gabby" Hayes and Pat Brady. Such script mishandling left Smiley just going along with the other players. Burnette does have humor as an Indian chief and hiding with Hayes in a fake horse skin. (A 65-minute version of HEART OF THE GOLDEN WEST has never been available, so Smiley's songs here, if any, are unknown.)

IDAHO (Republic, 1943). Smiley Burnette is in the groove once again as sidekick to State Ranger Roy Rogers. Here he's at Roy's side in bringing to justice two known criminals, Dick Purcell and Arthur Hohl, plus female nightclub owner Ona Munson, slyly attempting to blackmail local jurist Harry Shannon, who has a bank robber past. Smiley joins The Sons of the Pioneers on the tunes "Don Juan" and "Stop." Burnette does dances with Munson in one scene, then is captured by the perpetrators later, only to be set free by Shannon's boys' group.

(This was the first B-Western to play the prestigious Loew's chain of first-run theaters in New York. Deputy Roy Rogers and sidekick Smiley set out to prove a respected judge, who had once been a criminal, is being framed for crimes committed by a crooked saloon owner. With Roy, Smiley, The Sons of the Pioneers, Virginia Grey and Ona Munson, this film is a real winner.)

KING OF THE COWBOYS (Republic, 1943). With a World War II theme of destructive Nazi sabotage against various industries, rodeo performers Burnette and Roy Rogers go under cover at the behest of state governor Russell Hicks to halt perpetrators employed with a carnival show. Amongst the saboteurs are Gerald Mohr and James Bush, the latter a brother to actress Peggy Moran who forms a romantic attachment to Rogers. Smiley's humor includes washing dishes, a mind-reading act where he's almost electrocuted, and a disguise as Roy's grandpa. Burnette accompanies with "Ride 'em Cowboy" and "Ride, Ranger, Ride."

(After Autry entered the service, Republic spent a lot of money promoting Roy Rogers as their top Western star. According to a Variety *publicity release, Republic spent $500,000 in 1943 to promote Rogers. The campaign included billboards, radio spots, and heavy newspaper advertisements. The studio also came up with the idea for the film title, KING OF THE COWBOYS, making Roy the unofficial "King of the Cowboys." Since Autry had been the studio's No 1. star, and since he had been rated fourth on the 1942 list of top money-making Hollywood performers, it would have been Gene who would have starred in KING OF THE COWBOYS, and he would have assumed the "King" title.)*

SILVER SPURS (Republic, 1943). Having skipped Roy Rogers' previous B-Western, SONG OF TEXAS (Republic, 1943), Burnette returns here as Roy's steady partner one final time going in step with the star to prevent underhanded lodge owner John Carradine from seizing a railroad right-of-way across the ranch of murdered owner Jerome Cowan. Smiley has some good scenes with cohort Hal Taliaferro near a cliff, his constant complaining of a bad toothache, helping Roy force a confession from suspect Dick Wessel before he's slugged, and joining Rogers in a fast-moving carriage to defeat numerous bad guys on Kernville turf. (A 68-minute version of SILVER SPURS has never been available, so Smiley's songs here, if any, are unknown.)

BEYOND THE LAST FRONTIER (Republic, 1943). With Republic suddenly removing him from the higher-costing Roy Rogers musical horse operas, Smiley Burnette was inserted in the new studio *John Paul Revere* series with a historical setting. Burnette is co-starring beside Eddie Dew, both Texas Rangers, as they seek to rout notorious gun runners guided by veteran badman Harry Woods in the Old West. This very adept script was Smiley's first Republic B-Western away from the contemporary storyline in seven years. Burnette sings "Peg Leg Bandit" in the presence of young player Bob Mitchum, knocking him off a high-entrance walkway, but who later rescues Smiley from a barn blaze. Burnette even saves Dew from a runaway horse team. Although this is an Eddie Dew starring film, Mitchum steals the picture.

RAIDERS OF SUNSET PASS (Republic, 1943). It's back to the Modern Day West one last time for Smiley in his B-Western career as he joins forces again with Eddie Dew (John Paul Revere). Both Burnette and Dew are state cattle commission special investigators anxious to halt stock thieves raiding ranchers during World War II. They are assisted by the Women's Army of the Plains (WAPs) under command of leading lady Jennifer Holt to spot cattle rustlers in action, but the WAPs have uncheduled "accidents" caused by sneaks LeRoy Mason and Roy Barcroft. Smiley warbles "Who'd a Thunk It" and plays "One Man Glass Sympathy," and has a funny moment upon unintentionally falling from an attic.

PRIDE OF THE PLAINS (Republic, 1944). Republic switches from Eddie Dew to Bob Livingston as star of the *John Paul Revere* series with Burnette as a veterinarian/surgeon. He lends a hand to Livingston for this excellent oater in preventing the repeal of a law protecting wild horses which are being rustled off the range by outlaws Kenneth MacDonald and Yakima Canutt for profit. Burnette croons "Dr. Millhouse," a tune only heard in the full-length print of this B-Western. He has silliness "wiping off" paint from an odorous skunk which he thinks is a raccoon and does much saddle riding with Livingston in roping a pinto horse off the range only to wind up a foot later with aching bunions.

BENEATH WESTERN SKIES (Republic, 1944). Here was star Bob Livingston's last outing as John Paul Revere with Republic canceling any further B-Western screenplays of the law-and-order adventurer. Smiley's juvenile nephew Joe Strauch Jr., as Tadpole, is wasted for his brief acting moments. Movie momentum stops and starts too much although outdoor action is still good by Republic standards. Burnette is deputy sheriff to Livingston, brought in by past school teacher Effie Laird to stop a town gang of terrorists under orders from perennial owlhoot LeRoy Mason whom Burnette helps subdue by driving a wagon through the town bank's front entrance. Smiley, unfortunately, is weighed down by the script having him fiddle too much with wooden puppet Toad, dressed exactly like himself and Strauch along with a jail drunk. Burnette does considerable riding on horse Black-Eyed Nellie and manages to relax long enough to loudly warble "Travelin' Man" with Toad whom he bawls out before close of this movie's credits. Smiley and his disorganized comedy routines here mix like oil and water — not a good blend.

THE LARAMIE TRAIL (Republic, 1944). Smiley Burnette helps Bob Livingston end his excellent B-Western starring career at Republic on a very high plateau here as he joins Livingston in the mystery-oriented script involving stolen mine payroll funds and proving the innocence of young stranger John James accused of murder. In what was thought to be the start of a new studio B-Western series with Livingston as Johnny Rapidan, Smiley returns to true comedy form and generates good laughs gathering chicken eggs, wanting to trade knives with a Mexican lad, being gun-butted by murderer Bud Geary, and using his big stomach twice in different scenes to remove the smaller-built shyster legal eagle Emmett Lynn out of camera range. Burnette participates almost equally with Livingston in riding footage and warbles "Dish Rag Blues" (can only be heard by viewing a full-length print of THE LARAMIE TRAIL).

CALL OF THE ROCKIES (Republic, 1944). With the *John Paul Revere* series cancelled, Republic made Smiley Burnette star of his own B-*Superior Westerns* sagebrushers, and cast Sonny "Sunset" Carson as Burnette's saddle pal. This action-oriented horse opera, with a goodly amount of comedy, definitely proved that Burnette could handle a majority of acting scenes. He and Sunset tangle with crooked mining supplier Harry Woods and sneaky physician Frank Jaquet wanting to control all area mines. They also are at the side of engineer Kirk Alyn, the latter needing money desperately to improve underground shafts by rediverting water that leaks too much into the mines. Smiley's laugh times involve hearing and talking to Carson's horse Silver, being chewed out by Woods over stolen supplies, then later kissing him, posing as a bearded French engineer, and asking movie audiences to yell "bang" to gunman Henry Wills after running out of bullets to fire at the bad guy. Smiley warbles "T'aint Worth It."

(Smiley has a ridiculous part where he dons whiskers and poses as a French mining engineer. It is ludicrous to think the disguise would fool anyone.)

BORDERTOWN TRAIL (Republic, 1944). The "Sonny" part of Sunset Carson's name had been dropped effective with this B-oater's opening cast credits. Smiley and Sunset are border patrolmen battling smugglers Weldon Heyburn and Addison Richards attempting sneak-in of contraband gold worth $500,000 to the Republic of Texas to influence a negative vote against U. S. annexation. The smuggling is attempted through need of gun powder in a freight wagon and actual hauling of gold bars by stagecoach. Burnette has more woman problems — this time it's homely Ellen Lowe whose perfume-stained handkerchief he uses to wipe off a Border Patrol sign, only it erases some of the lettering. He also has to rough-tangle with gunman Jack Kirk and arm wrestle U. S. Army sergeant Rex Lease in a light moment. Most unusual here is the fact that former Columbia B-cowboy star Jack Luden portraying Carson's Army lieutenant brother, had his dialogue completely dubbed by character player Gayne Whitman, who was to have an unbilled feature role as a Communist years later in John Wayne's BIG JIM McLAIN (Warner Bros., 1952). After Burnette says that Luden doesn't know pigeon English, a parrot pipes in with: "So long, folks! That does it! Put on the newsreel!" Smiley croons on his beautiful "It's My Lazy Day."

CODE OF THE PRAIRIE (Republic, 1944). Smiley Burnette is a frustrated photographer who's both successful/unsuccessful at taking pictures. He and pal Sunset Carson chase off outlaws Rex Lease and Henry Wills after they've attacked the wagon of friends Peggy Stewart and Tom Chatterton, the latter an ex-lawman, arriving as a crusading news editor determined to bring justice to a frontier town. But Chatterton, after confronting smooth-talking barber Roy Barcroft as a wanted murderer, is knifed to death by Barcroft whose picture is accidentally taken by Burnette while he's moving the body. Smiley is chased away with gunfire from the scene by confederates Bud Geary and Tom London after they use him for a punching bag. Accused of Chatterton's murder, Sheriff Weldon Heyburn is proven innocent by Smiley because of the lawman's badge in a doctored photo. Burnette tells the theater audience: "You kids go home now. You've been in here all day." He also voices on "They Won't Pay Me."

FIREBRANDS OF ARIZONA (Republic, 1944). Smiley Burnette bows out of Republic B-Westerns here after nine straight years with this hilarious, all-fun feature. Smiley is a hypochondriac always worrying about his health by swallowing endless pills and to boot — a lazy hand on Peggy Stewart's ranch. Stewart, tired of such nonsense, fires Smiley, and has pal Sunset Carson take him to a medical clinic. But before both arrive at their destination, they are fired on by Sheriff Earle Hodgins and his posse plus Smiley's lookalike twin's gang belonging to Beefsteak Discoe. Arriving in the town of Medicine Springs brings endless mistaken identity for Burnette still thought of as Discoe. Everybody is afraid of Smiley, including a horse. With a net thrown over his head, Smiley/Discoe is in and out of jail for this feature's remainder. After Beefsteak steals $66,000 in reward money, Carson exposes this faker because he didn't want to swallow pills. In this B-Western, Burnette has humorous buckboard footage with player Tom London that energizes the screenplay's funniness, but has no songs.

(While some find this movie funny, others think it ridiculous and demeans the B-Western. At any rate, once you see this farce, you will not soon forget it. It is a Republic self-satire. An unusual Western played tongue-in-cheek and apparently released without fanfare.)

Once Smiley Burnette arrived at Columbia Pictures in early 1945 to eventually co-star beside studio veteran B-Western star Charles Starrett in *The Durango Kid* series, Smiley's sidekicking and comedy were to be severely limited by him and screenwriters in each sagebrusher except for a few pictures.

What follows is a listing of Burnette's films with Starrett naming only his on-screen occupations, the type of badmen involved with him, plus songs Smiley wrote and/or sang. However, the seven Columbia movies Burnette also filmed with saddlemate Gene Autry will be fully summarized as were his Republic oaters. Included are the music groups.

ROARING RANGERS (Columbia, 1946). Texas Ranger; ranch raiders; Merle Travis and His Bronco Busters; song — "Lazy Daily Dozen," "A New Ten Gallon Hat," and "The Old Chisholm Trail."

GUNNING FOR VENGEANCE (Columbia, 1946). Blacksmith; cattle rustlers; The Trailsmen; songs — "Smitty's a Liar," "Twenty Long Years," "Hominy Grits."

GALLOPING THUNDER (Columbia, 1946). Self-proclaimed expert; horse thieves; Merle Travis and His Bronco Busters; songs — "The Fife," "Getting Some Sleep," "The Wind Sings a Cowboy Song."

(Surprisingly, Val Kilmer (TOMBSTONE, 1993) was not the first to use the phrase "I'm your huckleberry." It was Smiley Burnette in this film.)

TWO-FISTED STRANGER (Columbia, 1946). Deputy sheriff; diamond swindlers; Zeke Clements of the Grand Old Opry; song — "Trombone Song."

THE DESERT HORSEMAN (Columbia, 1946). Cook; ranch thieves; Walt Shrum and His Colorado Hillbillies; songs — "He Was An Amateur Once," "Ring the Bell."

HEADING WEST (Columbia, 1946). Investigator; mine raiders; Hank Penny and His Plantation Boys; songs — "Scaredy Cat Blues," "That Old Ice Cream Freezer."

(This film has got to contain one of the most ridiculous scenes in a B-Western. When Smiley is captured by a gang of outlaws, there is a ludicrous scene where he sings one of his stupid songs ("Scaredy Cat Blues") to the crooks while they stand around and listen.)

LANDRUSH (Columbia, 1946). Dentist; terrorists; Ozie Waters and His Colorado Rangers; song — "Dentist Song."

TERROR TRAIL (Columbia, 1946). Peddler; range war instigators; Ozie Waters and His Colorado Rangers; songs — "Louisville Lady," "Way Down Low," "Peg Leg Bandit."

THE FIGHTING FRONTIERSMAN (Columbia, 1946). Ranger assistant; swindlers; Hank Newman and The Georgia Crackers; songs — "Swamp Woman Blues," "Don't Be Mad At Me," "Coyote Chorus."

SOUTH OF THE CHISHOLM TRAIL (Columbia, 1947). Medicine salesman; cattle rustlers; Hank Newman and The Georgia Crackers; songs — "King of Pain," "I'd Make a Hit With You," "I Got the Sillies," "Froggy Went A Courtin'."

(Smiley's a medicine show pitchman, but certainly not in the same league with Earle Hodgins.)

THE LONE HAND TEXAN (Columbia, 1947). Store clerk; oil well raiders; Mustard and Gravy; songs — "Smart Aleck Crow," "Never Say Love You On a Postcard," "What Makes You So Sweet?"

WEST OF DODGE CITY (Columbia, 1947). News printer; ranch intimidators; Mustard and Gravy; songs — "Can't Cry For Laughing," "Cricket Song."

(The attempt at comedy and songs by the duo Mustard and Gravy fail miserably — a total waste of film. Most of the cast and half the footage from this film show up again in Starrett's 1951 picture, BONANZA TOWN.)

LAW OF THE CANYON (Columbia, 1947). Prospector; supply wagon attackers; Texas Jim Lewis and His Lone Star Cowboys; songs — "Huntin' Trouble," "With My Luck," "If You Want to Be Happy."

(Smiley has come up with a gold/silver finding machine. Smiley describes Durango, "Boy, what a rootin'-tootin' he-catamount that galoot is!")

PRAIRIE RAIDERS (Columbia, 1947). Ranch foreman; horse rustlers; Ozie Waters and His Colorado Rangers; songs — "Thieving Burro," "Raisin' Rabbits."

THE STRANGER FROM PONCA CITY (Columbia, 1947). Café owner; cattle rustlers; Texas Jim Lewis and His Lone Star Cowboys; songs — "Catfish," "Law and Order," "Top It."

RIDERS OF THE LONE STAR (Columbia, 1947). Texas Ranger; mine attackers; Curly Williams and His Georgia Peach Pickers; songs — "Grandpa Frog," "Prairie Dog Lament," "Let Me By."

BUCKAROO FROM POWDER RIVER (Columbia, 1947). Barber; counterfeiters; Cass County Boys; songs — "Cecil Could See What He Wanted to See," "Sure Sounds Good to Me."

LAST DAYS OF BOOT HILL (Columbia, 1947). Deputy sheriff; ranch grabbers; Cass County Boys; song — "On My Way Back Home."

(Columbia again uses loads of stock footage from two 1945 Durango Westerns — BOTH BARRELS BLAZING and BLAZING THE WESTERN TRAIL.)

SIX-GUN LAW (Columbia, 1948). Photographer; extortionists; Curly Clements and His Rodeo Rangers; songs — "If I Were the Boss," "Around the Clock."

(Veteran character actor Hugh Prosser is the villain. Prosser was killed in an auto accident at Gallup, New Mexico in November 1952.)

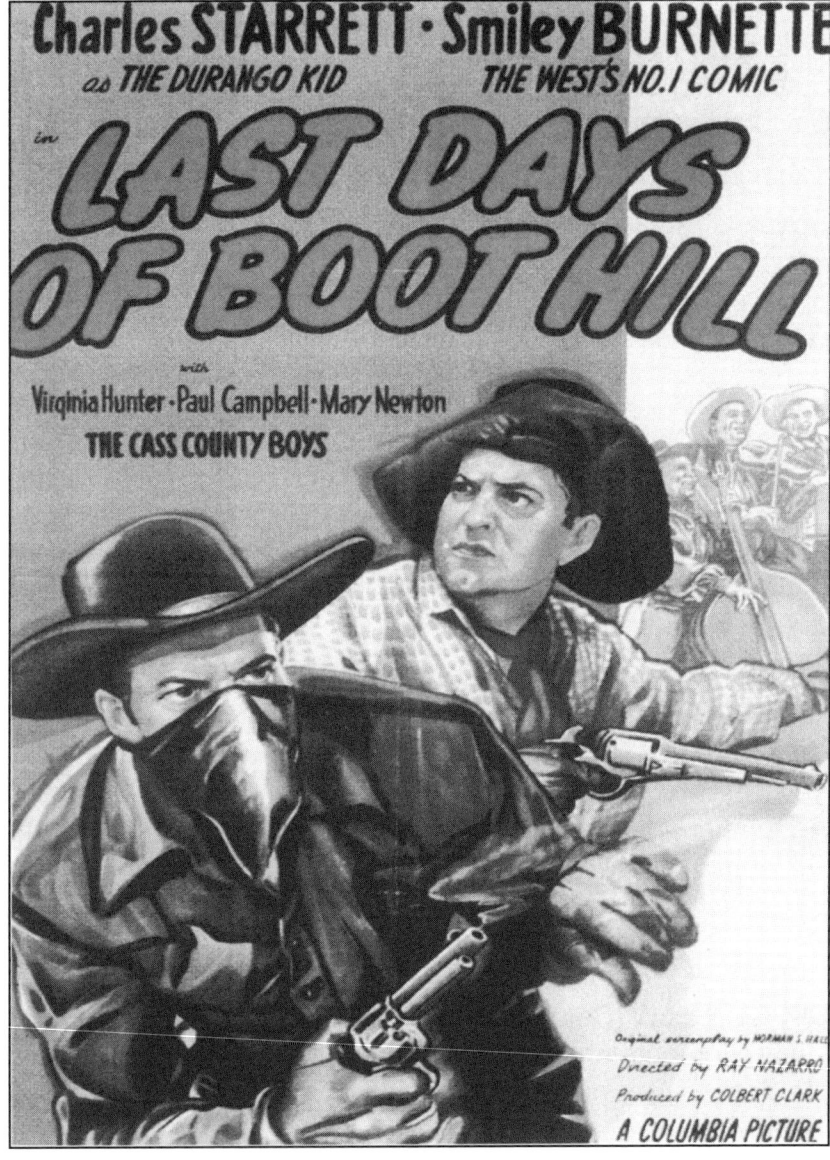

PHANTOM VALLEY (Columbia, 1948). Stable owner; land grabbers; Ozie Waters and His Colorado Rangers; song — "I'll Be Glad to See You."

WEST OF SONORA (Columbia, 1948). Touring actor; mine looters; The Sunshine Boys; songs — "Lil Indian," "I Ain't Gonna Do Tomorrow."

(When Smiley's female "star" fails to appear, Smiley dances in drag as Fifi LaTour.)

WHIRLWIND RAIDERS (Columbia, 1948). Itinerant tinker; corrupt state police; Doye O'Dell and The Radio Rangers; songs — "Fiddlin Fool," "Lookin' Poor, Feeling Rich."

(Smiley is a tinker — a traveling mender of metal household utensils — with a wagon and team of horses.)

BLAZING ACROSS THE PECOS (Columbia, 1948). Restaurant owner; Indian raiders; Red Arnall and His Western Aces; songs — "That's All Brother, That's All," "It Ain't Much Help."

Smiley and Steve Blake (Starrett) have the following dialogue:
Smiley: "That's a right nice horse there, ain't it?"
Steve: "It sure is! I wonder who he belongs to?"
Smiley: "Well, he belongs to Buckshot Thomas."
Steve: "Buckshot Thomas, eh? I don't think I know the gentleman."
Smiley: "Well, he ain't no gentleman."

TRAIL TO LAREDO (Columbia, 1948). Treasury Agent; gold smugglers; Cass County Boys; songs — "It's My Turn," "The Yodeler."

(Smiley performs a terribly unfunny scene. He goes wild with a paint brush while several men are playing poker. He sloshes paint all over the players, and they go right on with the game as if nothing is happening.)

EL DORADO PASS (Columbia, 1948). Saddle pal; coin robbers; Shorty Thompson and His Saddle Rockin' Rhythm; song — "Black, Black Jack of All Trades."

QUICK ON THE TRIGGER (Columbia, 1948). Saddle pal; stagecoach thieves; The Sunshine Boys; songs — "Bugle Boy," "Ring Eye Rhythm."

CHALLENGE OF THE RANGE (Columbia, 1949). Eastern author; cattlemen/farmer raiders; The Sunshine Boys; songs — "I Kin Dance," "My Home Town," "The More We Get Together."

DESERT VIGILANTE (Columbia, 1949). Ranch cook; silver smugglers; The Georgia Crackers; songs — "He Don't Like Work," "It Can't Be As Good As That."

LARAMIE (Columbia, 1949). Shoemaker; Indian troublemakers; no music group; songs — "Who Don't?", "The Happy Cobbler."

(A few minutes of stock footage is used from the 1939 United Artists movie, STAGECOACH. Starrett had to wear a shirt to match the one worn by John Wayne in that film. Stuntmen Yakima Canutt and Cliff Lyons, from STAGECOACH, are also both clearly visible.)

THE BLAZING TRAIL (Columbia, 1949). Newspaper editor; ranch seizers; Hank Penny and Slim Duncan; songs — "You Put Me On My Feet," "Extra, Extra!"

SOUTH OF DEATH VALLEY (Columbia, 1949). Lawman; mine thieves; Tommy Duncan and His All Western Stars; songs — "When You Go," "Ever Lovin' Marshal."

HORSEMEN OF THE SIERRAS (Columbia, 1949). Sheriff; ranch grabbers; T. Texas Tyler; song — "Tonight's My Night to Howl."

BANDITS OF EL DORADO (Columbia, 1949). Entertainer; criminal smugglers; Mustard and Gravy; songs — "The Rich Get Richer," "Tricky Senor."

RENEGADES OF THE SAGE (Columbia, 1949). Range rider; telegraph saboteurs; no music group; songs — "Pussy Foot," "Let Me Sleep."

TRAIL OF THE RUSTLERS (Columbia, 1950). Blacksmith; ranch seizers; Eddie Cletro and His Roundup Boys; songs — "Shoot Me Dead For That One," "I Should Say," "I Wish I'd Said That."

OUTCAST OF BLACK MESA (Columbia, 1950). Photographer; mine seizure; Ozie Waters; songs — "Donkey Engine," "Nobody Fires the Boss."

TEXAS DYNAMO (Columbia, 1950). Range pal; bank robbers; Slim Duncan; songs — "Fickle Finger of Fate," "Kitty Loved the Calliope."

STREETS OF GHOST TOWN (Columbia, 1950). Sidekick; gold robbers; Ozie Waters and His Colorado Rangers; song — "Streets of Laredo" (added Smiley Burnette lyrics).

(Smiley fears the strange happenings in a ghost town. Columbia really "cheats" the movie goers here with only about 20 feet of new film. The remaining footage is taken from two 1946 films in the series, GUNNING FOR VENGEANCE and LANDRUSH, with the latter dominating most of the running time.)

ACROSS THE BADLANDS (Columbia, 1950). Gunsmith; railroad attackers; Harmonica Bill; songs — "Harmonica Bill," "I'm Telling Myself I Ain't Afraid."

RAIDERS OF TOMAHAWK CREEK (Columbia, 1950). Correspondence school detective; ranch killers; no music group; songs — "I'm Too Smart For That," "The Grasshopper Polka."

LIGHTNING GUNS (Columbia, 1950). Bathtub salesman; dam site raiders; Ken Houchins; songs — "Bathtub Song," "Our Whole Family's Smart," "Ramblin' Blood In My Veins."

FRONTIER OUTPOST (Columbia, 1950). Range pal; gold raiders; Slim Duncan and Hank Penny; songs — "Twister," "Live to Eat."

PRAIRIE ROUNDUP (Columbia, 1951). Range pal; cattle thieves; The Sunshine Boys; songs — "Deep Froggy Blues," "Smack Happy."

(In an unusual turn-a-bout, Smiley bests badman John Cason in a fight scene. Undoubtedly, this would not have happened in real life since Cason was a former professional boxer.)

RIDIN' THE OUTLAW TRAIL (Columbia, 1951). Blacksmith; gold nugget swindlers; Pee Wee King and His Golden West Cowboys; songs — "I'm a Sucker For a Bargain," "Rackabye Baby."

FORT SAVAGE RAIDERS (Columbia, 1951). Range pal; terrorists against U. S. Army; no music group; song — "Full Steam Ahead."

SNAKE RIVER DESPERADOES (Columbia, 1951). Musician; Indian renegades; no music group; song — "Brass Band Polka."

(Smiley is hitting some sour notes with his trumpet and asked if he's getting paid to play: "No, I'm not getting paid for it, if that's what you mean ... but I'm just practicing. You know what they say about practice — practice makes perfect. Say, I wish you could hear the Smiley Burnette Silver Cornet Band. We can really play, I mean. I been all the way back to Indianapolis to get us some uniforms. Here, just look at that (as he pulls out a band hat). Boy, ain't that like downtown? Ain't that ritzy? Oh, I forgot, I was going to quit talking, wasn't I, so you could get some sleep.")

BONANZA TOWN (Columbia, 1951). Range pal; blackmailers; Slim Duncan; songs — "It All Goes to Show Ya," "Rooty Toot."

(It is outright cheating here as Columbia shot only about 30 minutes of new film and then padded the rest with footage taken from an earlier entry, WEST OF DODGE CITY.)

WHIRLWIND (Columbia, 1951). Smiley Burnette reunites as saddlemate with star Gene Autry together for a B-Western again after almost 8 1/2 years apart off screen. Burnette, as an

undercover veterinarian, joins postal inspector Autry to get the goods on big-time crook Thurston Hall who operates and uses his vast ranch as an outlaw syndicate front from which badmen proceed to pull off big-money raids. Smiley becomes involved with all-out humor while tussling against varmints Dick Curtis and Gregg Barton trying to stop Autry fist-whipping devious attorney Harry Lauter. Smiley also tangles with Sheriff Harry Harvey by roping his neck, wrist, and primitive wall phone plus becomes self-vaccinated while trying to tame a brahma bull calf for the medical feat. He and Autry happily warble "Tweedle-O-Twill."

CYCLONE FURY (Columbia, 1951). Range pal; horse thieves; Merle Travis and His Bronc Busters; song — "Trumpet Polka."

(Look for Louis Lettieri as the Indian kid. Lettieri played Little Beaver in the failed TV pilot Red Ryder *series, starring Allan Lane. And notice Clayton Moore. Moore had left* The Lone Ranger *TV series for more money. He would return to the role the following season.)*

THE KID FROM AMARILLO (Columbia, 1951). Treasury Agent; silver smugglers; Cass County Boys," song — "Great Burnette From Chihuahua."

PECOS RIVER (Columbia, 1951). Eyeglasses peddler; mail robbers; Harmonica Bill; songs — "The Eye Song," "Three Blind Mice," "Old Folks At Home" (Smiley Burnette's variations).

Memorable dialogue — Smiley says, "Whoa, whoa, whoa, Ringeye, whoa! Howdy, gentlemen. I'm Smiley Burnette, the eyeglass king, internationally known for Burnette's Better Bifocals. I'm a spec specialist, an eyeball mechanic, and a sight doc. What can I do for you gentlemen?"

SMOKY CANYON (Columbia, 1952). Range pal; cattle slaughterers; no music group; songs — "It's Got to Get Better Before It Gets Worse," "The Day Dream Lariat."

THE HAWK OF WILD RIVER (Columbia, 1952). Range pal; gold thieves; no music group; songs — "Chief Pocatello From the Cherokees," "Pedro Enchilada."

Durango and Smiley are sent to Wild River to recover a gold shipment that has been stolen by the Hawk (Clayton Moore) and his gang.

LARAMIE MOUNTAINS (Columbia, 1952). U S. Army cook; gold raiders; no music group; song — "Sloop, Sloop, Sloop."

(Smiley is not at his best here. His antics appear more like a spoiled kid seeking attention. He is an Army sergeant and the fort's cook. In this film he has a dog called Ringeye.)

THE ROUGH, TOUGH WEST (Columbia, 1952). Fire chief; mine swindlers; Pee Wee King and His Band; song — "Fire of Forty-One."

JUNCTION CITY (Columbia, 1952). Range pal; gold mine grabbers; no music group; song — "Lil' Injun."

THE KID FROM BROKEN GUN (Columbia, 1952). Range pal; gold coin robbers; no music group; song — "It's the Law."

(Charles Starrett ends his movie career with this picture. Starrett's favorite feature wasn't among the Durangos he made, but rather the earlier OUTLAWS OF THE PRAIRIE (Columbia, 1937) where Charles' character as a younger person had a finger maimed by his father's murderer. Such

information was revealed by veteran B-Western enthusiast Mack A. Houston who heard Starrett divulge this fact while a guest celebrity at the 1980 Memphis Film Festival.)

WINNING OF THE WEST (Columbia, 1953). Smiley Burnette, with *The Durango Kid* series filming permanently ended by early April 1952, rejoins cowboy star Gene Autry as sidekick almost three months later for the singer's last six Columbia B-Westerns. Smiley is a printer at Gene's side as he's ousted from the Territorial Rangers following Autry's questionable response during the fatal shooting of news publisher William Forrest. The murder victim was shot by Autry outlaw brother Richard Crane, who later captures Smiley and Gene under the watchful eye of ruthless gang lead Robert Livingston, proud of his Indian raids that have garnered vast amounts of loot. Having a change of heart, Crane instigates freedom for Autry and Burnette with the brother then gunned down by Livingston, with the latter and his gang later captured in a running gun battle. Smiley has fun with female lead Gail Davis when he shows her his bag of tricks during a stagecoach ride and humorously relates to Sheriff House Peters, Jr. about an attempted heist. Burnette sings "Five Minutes Late and a Dollar Short" plus "Fetch Me Down My Trusty .45" with Autry.

ON TOP OF OLD SMOKY (Columbia, 1953). Smiley has a self-proclaimed girl friend in leading lady Gail Davis, the operator of a toll road. Someone is trying to wreck Davis' enterprise which turns out to be underhanded eyeglassses' store owner Grandon Rhodes and bullies Robert Bice and Zon Murray who've discovered valuable mica deposits on her property. Pretending to be a Texas Ranger, Gene Autry saddles next to Smiley in smashing the miscreants' scheme by first fighting both Bice and Murray. Smiley comically encounters the latter bad guy during this melee and breaks The Cass County Boys from jail by digging a tunnel in the midst of a rainstorm. Burnette croons "Hang My Head and Cry" plus "I Saw Her First."

GOLDTOWN GHOST RIDERS (Columbia, 1953). As a hauler of explosives, Smiley Burnette finds himself plenty scared of such cargo plus "ghost riders" in this confusing oater saga while pal Gene Autry takes to the saddle as a circuit judge. Outlaws use the rider images to loot gold claims while Smiley has abundant comedy segments trying to rescue pretty Gail Davis, whose carriage becomes stuck in a stream only to fall in the water, a powder keg chases him, etc. Claim jumper Denver Pyle steals Burnette's explosives to pile down rocks on a wagon train. During the frantic times, Burnette sings and dances to "Pancho's Widow" and makes ice cream while warbling "The Thieving Burro."

(This film contains stock footage from RIDERS IN THE SKY (Columbia, 1949) and THE BIG SOMBRERO (Columbia, 1949). Like practically all the Western sidekicks, Smiley is afraid of ghosts and issues the following warning: "Well, I just wouldn't want to scare you, lady. Nobody's ever seen 'em ... that is close, anyhow. Ever so often they come riding out of Ghost Canyon, up there where there's mists and clouds. If you look, you can see right now. Down out of their hidden canyons they come, like they was riding out of another world. Protecting their hidden gold, that's why they're haunting us — keeping gold-hungry miners from digging up their graves. Look at 'em, their blood gone from their veins, their eyes cold as death, and them ghost-like horses — they don't even leave hoof prints you can ever find. I reckon you've heard of miners and prospectors disappearing in the hills. That's what's happened to 'em — the riders got 'em ... gone without a trace. You'll never hear of 'em again. You get the feeling they ride past like a cold wind that goes right through you, giving you the creeps and the shivers while they disappear back where they came from. And then when you look around, they're gone.")

PACK TRAIN (Columbia, 1953). It's literally a tough trail to hoe for Burnette while saddling alongside partner Autry in delivering much needed food/medicine supplies to awaiting settlers. Smiley warns Gene that saloon proprietor Kenne Duncan and storekeeper Sheila Ryan are selling Autry's $5,000 worth of pre-purchased supplies for his trusting citizens to gold miners at hiked prices to make excess profit. Smiley and Gene ward off Duncan and his gunmen with numerous shooting scrapes plus dodging an avalanche of explosive rockslides. With the dying of a small girl back in camp, Autry becomes more determined to corral Duncan, the latter whom he pummels on a runaway train. For the funny times, Smiley gets pelted with endless tomatoes by Ryan, is drowned with water from a barrel, and falls down an embankment chasing youngster B. G. Norman. Burnette sings "Hominy Grits" and "Wagon Train."

(The film's ending contains stock footage from Gene's THE BLAZING SUN (Columbia, 1950). Earlier scenes also have been excerpted from Autry's THE BIG SOMBRERO (Columbia, 1949)).

SAGINAW TRAIL (Columbia, 1953). Smiley's an undercover trapper, actually a Hamilton Ranger, keeping an eye on events at hand until fellow lawman Gene Autry arrives to work hand-in-hand with Burnette to halt murderous Indians and renegade whites from attacking incoming Michigan settlers. French-trapper king Eugene Borden and subordinate Myron Healey resent intrusion on their rich animal territory, thus the continuing warfare. Burnette's humorous sequences are confined here, but one comic event occurs for him by lifting a big keg to impress other trappers. Smiley croons "Mam'selle."

LAST OF THE PONY RIDERS (Columbia, 1953). Trail's end on the movie screen after 19 years with faithful saddle pal Gene Autry, plus Roy Rogers, Eddie Dew, Bob Livingston, Sunset Carson, and Charles Starrett has arrived for Smiley Burnette. Autry decided to end his B-Western acting here with the ever encroaching medium of television to devote his talents to this medium plus continue his Flying A Pictures production company for 30-minute TV shows that he established in 1950. For Gene's swan song of the Pony Express resisting an approaching stageline franchise to deliver mail, Burnette has an easy goodbye to those many devoted fans with only a couple of scenes that include climbing a telegraph pole, being a cook, and rescuing Autry after his detainment by conniving banker Howard Wright's attempt to sneakily win the mail-hauling contract with the Pony Express demise. Easier than comedy, all Smiley has to do is smile and eat chicken legs, plus warble "Sugar Babe" alongside Gene.

Smiley met Elvis Presley, probably sometime in the early to mid-1960s. No doubt a treat for both entertainers.

DUAL ROLES

Several cowboy stars play dual roles. Sidekicks Smiley, Max Terhune, and Fuzzy St. John did also. Here is a list of the heroes that played dual roles.

Thanks to Les Adams

The Hero in Dual Roles — Westerns & Serials

Release Date	Title	Company	Who	Dual Roles
3/15/31	RIVER'S END, THE	Warners	Charles Bickford	RCMP Sgt. Derry Conniston and John Keith
12/6/31	POCATELLO KID, THE	Tiffany	Ken Maynard	The Pocatello Kid and Jim Bledsoe
4/16/34	HONOR OF THE RANGE	Universal	Ken Maynard	Ken Bellamy and Clem Bellamy
2/1/35	PHANTOM COWBOY, THE	Aywon	Ted Wells	Bill Collins and Jim Russell
2/13/35	WILDERNESS MAIL	Ambassador	Kermit Maynard	Rance Raine and Keith Raine
7/1/35	BRANDED A COWARD	Supreme	Johnny Mack Brown	Johnny Hume and Bill "The Cat" Hume

Date	Title	Studio	Star	Characters
8/1/35	TOMBSTONE TERROR	Supreme	Bob Steele	Duke Dixon and Jimmy Dixon
12/30/35	BULLDOG COURAGE	Puritan	Tim McCoy	Tim Braddock and Slim Braddock
12/30/35	CUSTERS LAST STAND (Serial)	Stage and Screen	Rex Lease	Kit Cardigan and John Cardigan
1/2/36	DESERT GUNS	Beaumont	Conway Tearle	Kirk Allenby and Bob Enright
11/16/36	BIG SHOW, THE	Republic	Gene Autry	Gene Autry and Tom Ford
12/1/36	BOSS RIDER OF GUN CREEK	Universal	Buck Jones	Larry Day and Gary Elliott
4/1/37	FEUD OF THE TRAIL, THE	Victory	Tom Tyler	Tom Wade and Jack Granger
8/27/37	TRAILING TROUBLE	Grand National	Ken Maynard	"Friendly" Fields and Blackie Burke
9/1/37	MOONLIGHT ON THE RANGE	Spectrum	Fred Scott	Jeff Peters and Killer Dane
4/14/38	OUTLAWS OF SONORA	Republic	Bob Livingston	Stony Brooke and Dude Brannen
5/1/38	TWO-GUN MAN FROM HARLEM	Merit/Sack	Herbert Jeffrey	Bob Blake and The Deacon
9/16/38	BILLY THE KID RETURNS	Republic	Roy Rogers	Roy Rogers and Billy the Kid
9/16/38	BLACK BANDIT	Universal	Bob Baker	Bob Ramsay and Don Ramsay
3/5/39	TWO GUN TROUBADOR	Spectrum	Fred Scott	Fred Dean Sr. and Jr.
4/19/39	OUTLAW'S PARADISE	Victory	Tim McCoy	"Lightnin' Bill" Carson and Trigger Mallory
5/12/39	THREE TEXAS STEERS	Republic	Ray Corrigan	Tucson Smith and "The Gorilla"
8/12/39	STRAIGHT SHOOTER	Victory	Tim McCoy	"Lightnin' Bill" Carson and Sam Brown

5/24/40	ROCKY MOUNTAIN RANGERS	Republic	Bob Livingston	Stony Brooke and The Laredo Kid
5/31/40	BAD MAN FROM RED BUTTE	Universal	Johnny Mack Brown	Buck Halliday and Gils Brady
6/19/40	WAGONS WESTWARD	Republic	Chester Morris	David Cook and Tom Cook
8/10/40	RIVER'S END, THE	Warners	Dennis Morgan	Sergeant Derry Conniston and John Keith
4/10/41	TWO GUN SHERIFF	Republic	Don Barry	Sheriff Bruce McKinnon and Jim "Sundown" McKinnon
8/29/41	LONE RIDER AMBUSHED, THE	P.R.C.	George Houston	Tom Cameron (The Lone Rider) and Keno Harris
10/17/41	DRIFTIN' KID, THE	Monogram	Tom Keene	Tom Sterling and Jim Vernon
10/18/41	JESSE JAMES AT BAY	Republic	Roy Rogers	Jesse James and Clint Burns
12/18/41	RIDERS OF THE BADLANDS	Columbia	Charles Starrett	Steve Langdon and Mac Collins
2/12/42	BULLETS FOR BANDITS	Columbia	Bill Elliott	Wild Bill Hickok and Prince Katey
8/21/42	LAW AND ORDER	P.R.C.	Buster Crabbe	Billy the Kid and Lt. Ted Morrison
9/4/42	ARIZONA STAGECOACH	Monogram	Ray Corrigan	Crash Corrigan (I) and Crash Corrigan (2)
9/4/42	ARIZONA STAGECOACH	Monogram	John King	Dusty King (I) and Dusty King (2)
9/4/42	ARIZONA STAGECOACH	Monogram	Max Terhune	Alibi Terhune (1) and Alibi Terhune (2)
10/2/42	SHERIFF OF SAGE VALLEY	P.R.C.	Buster Crabbe	Billy the Kid and Ed "Kansas Ed" Bonney

Date	Title	Studio	Star	Character(s)
4/29/43	CHEYENNE ROUNDUP	Universal	Johnny Mack Brown	Buck Brandon and Gils Brandon
7/1/43	FUGITIVE FROM SONORA	Republic	Don Barry	Ted Winters (Keeno Phillips) and Parson Dave Winters
8/24/43	SHADOWS ON THE SAGE	Republic	Bob Steele	Tucson Smith and Curley
9/7/43	TRAIL OF TERROR	P.R.C.	Dave O'Brien	Ranger Tex Wyatt and Curly Wyatt
6/14/44	DRIFTER, THE	P.R.C.	Buster Crabbe	Billy Carson and Drifter Davis
9/15/44	STAGECOACH TO MONTEREY	Republic	Allan Lane	Bruce Redmond and Chick Weaver
4/20/45	CORPUS CHRISTI BANDITS	Republic	Allan Lane	Captain James Christi and Corpus Christi Jim
11/7/45	PRAIRIE RUSTLERS	P.R.C.	Buster Crabbe	Billy Carson and Jim Slade
3/8/47	GUNSMOKE	Standard Pictures/ Astor	Nick Stuart	Brad Marlowe and Mr. Marlowe
6/17/48	TIOGA KID, THE	P.R.C.	Eddie Dean	Eddie Dean and Clip (Tioga Kid) Mason
1/7/49	OUTLAW COUNTRY	Screen Guild	Lash LaRue	Marshal Lash LaRue and The Frontier Phantom
7/1/49	TRAIL OF THE MOUNTIES	Screen Guild	Russell Hayden	Sandy Sanderson and Johnny Sanderson
7/1/49	RIM OF THE CANYON	Columbia	Gene Autry	Gene Autry and his father
8/12/50	GUNFIRE	Lippert	Don Barry	Frank James and Bat Fenton
2/1/52	FRONTIER PHANTOM, THE	West. Adv.	Lash LaRue	Marshal Lash LaRue and The Frontier Phantom
3/27/53	SON OF THE RENEGADE	United Artists	Johnny Carpenter	Red River Johnny Sr. and Jr.

Release Date	Title	Company	Who	Dual Roles
7/1/54	LAWLESS RIDER, THE	United Artists	Johnny Carpenter	John Carpenter and Rod Tatum
9/25/56	FLESH AND THE SPUR	Amer. -Int.	John Agar	Luke Random and Matt Random
7/1/65	CAT BALLOU	Columbia	Lee Marvin	Tim Strawn and Kid Shilleen

The Heroine, Sidekick, Second Lead in Dual Roles

Release Date	Title	Company	Who	Dual Roles
12/1/44	FIREBRANDS OF ARIZONA	Republic	Smiley Burnette	Frog Millhouse and Beefsteak Discoe
2/3/45	HIS BROTHER'S GHOST	P.R.C.	Al St. John	Fuzzy Jones and Andy Jones
9/29/45	SUNSET IN EL DORADO	Republic	Dale Evans	Kansas Kate Wiley and Lucille Wiley
11/18/46	STARS OVER TEXAS	P.R.C.	Lee Bennett	Bert Ford and Waco

Dual roles by the numbers: Buster Crabbe (4), Ken Maynard (3), Don Barry (3), Johnny Mack Brown (3), Allan Lane (2), Robert Livingston (2), Fred Scott (2), Gene Autry (2), Roy Rogers (3), Tim McCoy (2), Ray Corrigan (2), Lash LaRue (2) and Bob Steele (2). These played dual roles only once: George Houston, Charles Starrett, Bill Elliott, Tom Keene, Dusty King, Eddie Dean, Buck Jones, Rex Lease, Ted Wells and Bob Baker.

OBITUARY

SMILEY BURNETTE
Of 'Autry' Fame
Succumbs At 55

(This report came from The Associated Press, and some of the information may be incorrect or duplicated in the previous text.)

ENCINO, Calif. A musical saw and an accordion boosted Smiley Burnette to success as a comic with Gene Autry and other Western stars during a career which he had made 171 pictures up until his death Thursday night.

Smiley, whose checkered shirt and tattered cowboy hat were familiar to thousands of theater-goers, succumbed to leukemia, friends said. He was 55 and had been under hospital treatment since February 8.

During his heyday of Westerns, Burnette was one of the top money-making performers, appearing in the 1930s and 1940s with Autry, Roy Rogers and others. In recent years he appeared in television most recently as the railroad engineer in "Petticoat Junction.

Thirty years ago Burnette was performing with saw and sqeeze-box for a radio station in Tuscaloosa, Illinois, shortly after finishing high school. After a long series of radio and personal appearances with Autry, Burnette made 57 movies with the star.

When television's impact impeded Western films, Burnette retired temporarily then emerged for personal appearances. He wrote 353 Western tunes during his career and made innumerable appearances from refreshment stand roofs to drive-in theaters and shopping centers. At last he, too, joined the television clan.

SELECTED BIBLIOGRAPHY

Rothel, David, *Those Great Cowboy Sidekicks*
Rothel, David, *The Gene Autry Book*
Magers, Boyd, *Gene Autry Westerns*
Magers, Boyd, various issues of *Western Clippings*
Anderson, Chuck, The Old Corral website
Autry, Gene, *Back In the Saddle Again*
Herskowitz, Mickey, *Back In the Saddle Again*
Mathis, Jack, *Republic Confidential — The Studio*
Mathis, Jack, *Republic Confidential — The Players*
Smith, John Guyot, article in *Gene Autry's Friends*
Pando, Leo, article in *The Old Cowboy Picture Show*
Miller, Don, *Hollywood Corral*
McCord, Merrill, *Brothers of the West —The Lives and Films of Robert Livingston and Jack Randall*
Carmen, Bob and Scapperotti, Dan, *The Adventures of the Durango Kid*
Tuska, Jon, *The Filming of the West*
Green, Douglas B., *Singing In the Saddle*
Copeland, Bobby, *Trail Talk*
Copeland, Bobby, *B-Western Boot Hill*
Wollstein, Hans, *All-Movie Guide*
George-Warren, Holly, *Public Cowboy No. 1 — The Life and Times of Gene Autry*

ABOUT THE AUTHORS

Reared in Oak Ridge, Tennessee, Bobby Copeland began going to the Saturday matinee B-Western movies at nearby theaters. He was immediately impressed by the moral code of these films and has tried to pattern his life after the examples set by the cowboy heroes. After graduating from high school and attending Carson-Newman College and the University of Tennessee, he set out to raise a family and start a career at the Oak Ridge National Laboratory. His love for the old Western films was put on the shelf and lay dormant for some 35 years. One Saturday, in the mid-1980s, he happened to turn on his television, and the station was showing a Lash LaRue movie. This rekindled his interest. He contacted the TV program's host ("Marshal" Andy Smalls) and was invited to appear on the program. Since that time, Bobby has had some 100 articles published, written 12 books, contributed to some 20 books, made several speeches, appeared on television over 40 times, and has been interviewed by several newspapers and four independent radio stations as well as the Public Radio Broadcasting System to provide commentary and promote interest in B-Western films. In 1985 he was a co-founder of the Knoxville, Tennessee-based "Riders of the Silver Screen Club," serving five times as president. He initiated and edited the club's newsletter for several years.

In 1996, Bobby's first book, *Trail Talk*, was published by Empire Publishing, Inc. (one of the world's largest publishers of books on Western films and performers). It was followed by *B-Western Boot Hill*, *Bill Elliott — The Peaceable Man*, *Roy Barcroft — King of the Badmen*, *Charlie King — We Called Him Blackie*, *Silent Hoofbeats*, *Johnny Mack Brown — Up Close and Personal*, *Sunset Carson — The Adventures of a Cowboy Hero*, and *Best of the Badmen* by Boyd Magers, Bob Nareau, and Bobby. In addition to these popular books, Bobby also self-published *The Bob Baker Story*, *The Whip Wilson Story*, and *Five Heroes*. He has attended some 60

Western film festivals, and has met many of the Western movie performers. He continues to contribute articles to the various Western magazines, and he is a regular columnist for Western Clippings. In 1988, Bobby received the "Buck Jones Rangers Trophy," presented annually to individuals demonstrating consistent dedication to keeping the spirit of the B-Western alive. In 1994, Don Key (Empire Publishing) and Boyd Magers (Video West, Inc. & *Western Clippings*) awarded Bobby the "Buck Rainey Shoot-em-Ups Pioneer Award," which yearly honors a fan who has made significant contributions towards the preservation of interest in the B-Westerns. In 2006, he received the "Saddle Pal Award," presented by the *Old Cowboy Picture Show* Magazine, and in 2007, he was honored with the "Edward A. Wall Memorial Award" by the Williamsburg Film Festival. Bobby has been featured on two DVDs — one about the history of B-Western films, and another about the life of Dub Taylor.

Bobby is an active member at Oak Ridge's Central Baptist Church. He retired in 1996 after 40 years at the same workplace. Bobby plans to continue his church work, write more B-Western articles, and enjoy his retirement with his faithful sidekick, Joan.

Bobby Copeland

Richard B. Smith, III is a retired writer and editor whose devotion to the B-Western genre began around 1949 when at age 8 he made occasional Saturday-matinee visits to see Gene Autry and Roy Rogers in their musical horse operas at the small Pitts-Clarco Theater in Berryville, Virginia. Further knowledge for young Richard about these features accelerated by the time he saw old B-Westerns simultaneously on television beginning in August 1951.

In 1958, Smith commenced serious research for film credits on shoot-em-up stars by constantly perusing old movie display ads from newspaper morgues of northwestern Virginia and far eastern West Virginia. Over the last four decades, he has scanned film books, files and trade papers such as *Variety* and *The Hollywood Reporter* at the Library of Congress.

Richard worked for the late Jack Mathis (from 1980 to 1982) whose "Republic Confidential" project required him to compile a super-index of credits on Republic Pictures (1935-1959) players and technical personnel which was done from October 2, 1980 through April 21, 1981 over a 202-day period. For Mathis, he also photo copied 25 years of *Variety* microfilm articles on Republic plus assembled a trade papers compendium. Smith's uncredited work was published in two Mathis books — *Republic Confidential (Vol. 1 —The Studio, 1999 and Vol. 2 — The Players, 1992)*.

Richard authored "B-Westerns in Perspective" beginning in 1978 for *The Big Reel,* then as a separate publication and later during 1989 for *Under Western Skies*, with each highlighted movie having data on filming dates, locations, production criteria, etc. He also contributed the same format in columns for *Western Clippings* (1994-2002) titled "Behind the Cameras."

Smith was co-author with John Rutherford on *Cowboy Shooting Stars* (1988) and on the expanded *More Cowboy Shooting Stars* (1992).

During 2006-2007, Richard was editorial assistant on Boyd

Magers' *Gene Autry Westerns* (2007). He also offered editorial assistance on former B-Western actor House Peters, Jr.'s autobiography, *Another Side of Hollywood* (2001) and Merrill McCord's *Brothers of the West: The Lives and Films of Robert Livingston and Jack Randall* (2003).

In recent years, Richard has lent editorial help also on prolific writer Bobby Copeland's many publications: *The Bob Baker Story, The Whip Wilson Story, Five Heroes* (all in 1998), *B-Western Boot Hill* (1999), *Bill Elliott — The Peaceable Man* (2000), *Roy Barcroft — King of the Badmen* (2000), *Silent Hoofbeats* (2001), *Charlie King — We Called Him Blackie* (2003), and *Johnny Mack Brown — Up Close and Personal* (2005). In 1999, Richard was the 9th and last recipient of the "Buck Rainey Shoot-Em-Ups Pioneer Award" which recognized his literary contributions.

Richard B. Smith, III

Smith is a 1963 B.A. graduate of Shepherd University, Shepherdstown, West Virginia, having majored in English with a minor in Journalism.

Other Fine Western Books Available from Empire Publishing, Inc:

ABC's of Movie Cowboys by Edgar M. Wyatt. $5.00.
Art Acord and the Movies by Grange B. McKinney. $15.00.
Audie Murphy: Now Showing by Sue Gossett. $30.00.
Back in the Saddle: Essays on Western Film and Television Actors edited by Garry Yoggy. $29.95.
Best of the Badmen by Boyd Magers, Bobby Copeland, and Bob Nareau. $39.00.
Bill Elliott, The Peaceable Man by Bobby Copeland. $15.00.
Brothers of the West: The Lives and Films of Robert Livingston and Jack Randall by Merrill McCord. $34.95.
B-Western Boot Hill: A Final Tribute to the Cowboys and Cowgirls Who Rode the Saturday Matinee Movie Range by Bobby Copeland
B-Western Actors Encyclopedia by Ted Holland. $30.00.
Buster Crabbe, A Self-Portrait as told to Karl Whitezel. $24.95.
B-Western Boot Hill: A Final Tribute to the Cowboys and Cowgirls Who Rode the Saturday Matinee Movie Range by Bobby Copeland. $15.00.
Charlie King: We Called Him Blackie by Bobby Copeland. $15.00.
The Cowboy and the Kid by Jefferson Brim Crow, III. $5.90.
Crusaders of the Sagebrush by Hank Williams. $29.95.
Duke, The Life and Image of John Wayne by Ronald L. Davis. $14.95.
The Films and Career of Audie Murphy by Sue Gossett. $18.00.
The First Fifty Years of Sound Western Movie Locations by Kenny Stier. $34.95.
Gene Autry Westerns — America's Favorite Cowboy by Boyd Magers. $45.00.
The Golden Corral, A Roundup of Magnificent Western Films by Ed Andreychuk. $29.95.
The Hollywood Posse, The Story of a Gallant Band of Horsemen Who Made Movie History by Diana Serra Cary. $16.95.
Hoppy by Hank Williams. $29.95.
In a Door, Into a Fight, Out a Door, Into a Chase, Movie-Making Remembered by the Guy at the Door by William Witney. $24.95.
John Ford, Hollywood's Old Master by Ronald L. Davis. $14.95.
John Wayne—Actor, Artist, Hero by Richard D. McGhee. $27.50.
John Wayne, An American Legend by Roger M. Crowley. $29.95.
Johnny Mack Brown—Up Close and Personal by Bobby Copeland. $20.00.
Kid Kowboys: Juveniles in Western Films by Bob Nareau. $20.00.
Ladies of the Western by Boyd Magers and Michael G. Fitzgerald. $35.00.
Lash LaRue, King of the Bullwhip by Chuck Thornton and David Rothel. $25.00.
Last of the Cowboy Heroes by Budd Boetticher. $28.50.
More Cowboy Shooting Stars by John A. Rutherford and Richard B. Smith, III. $18.00.
The Official TV Western Roundup Book by Neil Summers and Roger M. Crowley. $34.95.
Randolph Scott, A Film Biography by Jefferson Brim Crow, III. $25.00.
Richard Boone: A Knight Without Armor in a Savage Land by David Rothel. $30.00.
Riding the (Silver Screen) Range, The Ultimate Western Movie Trivia Book by Ann Snuggs. $15.00.
Riding the Video Range, The Rise and Fall of the Western on Television by Garry A. Yoggy. $75.00.
The Round-Up, A Pictorial History of Western Movie and Television Stars Through the Years by Donald R. Key. $27.00.
Roy Rogers, A Biography, Radio History, Television Career Chronicle, Discography, Filmography, etc. by Robert W. Phillips. $75.00.
Roy Barcroft: King of the Badmen by Bobby Copeland. $15.00.
The Roy Rogers Reference-Trivia-Scrapbook by David Rothel. $25.00.
Saddle Gals, A Filmography of Female Players in B-Westerns of the Sound Era by Edgar M. Wyatt and Steve Turner. $10.00.
Silent Hoofbeats: A Salute to the Horses and Riders of the Bygone B-Western Era by Bobby Copeland. $20.00.
Singing in the Saddle by Douglas B. Green. $34.95.
Sixty Great Cowboy Movie Posters by Bruce Hershenson. $14.99.
The Sons of the Pioneers by Bill O'Neal and Fred Goodwin. $26.95.
So You Wanna See Cowboy Stuff? by Boyd Magers. $25.00.
Sunset Carson — The Adventures of a Cowboy Hero by Bobby J. Copeland and Richard B. Smith, III. $18.00.
Tex Ritter: America's Most Beloved Cowboy by Bill O'Neal. $21.95.
Those Great Cowboy Sidekicks by David Rothel. $25.00.
Trail Talk, Candid Comments and Quotes by Performers and Participants of The Saturday Matinee Western Films by Bobby Copeland. $12.50.
The Western Films of Sunset Carson by Bob Carman and Dan Scapperotti. $20.00.
Western Movies: A TV and Video Guide to 4200 Genre Films compiled by Michael R. Pitts. $35.00.
Westerns Women by Boyd Magers and Michael G. Fitzgerald. $35.00.
Written, Produced, and Directed by Oliver Drake. $30.00.

Ask for our complete listing of WESTERN MOVIE BOOKS!

Add $4.00 shipping/handling for first book + $1.00 for each additional book ordered.
Empire Publishing, Inc. • 3130 US Highway 220 • Madison, NC 27025-8706 • Phone 336-427-5850